The

BUSY WOMAN'S GUIDE *to*

WRITING *a*

WORLD-CHANGING

BOOK

OTHER WORKS BY CYNTHIA MORRIS

Create Your Writer's Life: A Guide to Writing with Joy and Ease

Creative Toolkit for Travelers

Leading Tours for Fun and Profit

*Cross the Finish Line: Overcome the Hurdles to
Completing Your Projects*

*The Graceful Return: Relish Your Journey After
You have Come Home*

Chasing Sylvia Beach

*Visit Paris Like an Artist:
Have More Fun and Creative Adventures in the City of Light*

The

BUSY WOMAN'S GUIDE *to*

WRITING *a*

WORLD-CHANGING

BOOK

BY

CYNTHIA
MORRIS

Original Impulse, Inc.
Copyright © 2019 by Cynthia L. Morris
LIBRARY OF CONGRESS CATALOGING-IN-
PUBLICATION DATA
Library of Congress Control Number: 2019930161

ISBN 9780975922477 (paperback)
       0975922483 (e-book)

Set in Hoefler Text
Designed by *the*BookDesigners

∽ DEDICATION ∽

Here's to the people who are bravely bringing their words to the page. Keep opening your heart, uncapping your pen and sharing your brilliance. The world needs it.

᠃ CONTENTS ᠃

INTRODUCTION

Hello! I am so happy you are reading this. It means you are taking steps to fulfill what may be a lifelong dream—to write a book. You have a message, work or story that must be shared, and you want to write the book that only *you* can write.

You are smart, you have something to say and you are ready to put it into form. And because you care deeply about your subject, you may be plagued with doubts and insecurities along the way. This happens to each and every one of us as we move closer to getting our ideas out of our head and onto paper.

You are also busy with your other roles. Chances are you are a mother and the head of your household. You run the ship—keeping food in the fridge, making sure everyone's clothes are clean and presentable, ensuring that the bills get paid, the kids get to their activities, and that everything hums along seamlessly. If you aren't doing all this yourself, you are responsible for hiring the help to make everything happen.

Perhaps you work outside the home. You are a career woman who has as many responsibilities at work as you do at home. It might seem impossible to write a book alongside all your other obligations. Yet you also know that it *has to happen.* Your big idea keeps pestering you like another child that needs attention.

For over two decades, I have been helping women just like you bring their books into the world. I have written eight books of my own and coached hundreds of writers to find their seat and write their words. I know the challenges you face to carve out time to write. Even though there are days when it seems your book is as far away as the summit of Mount Everest, I am certain it's possible to write the book that's inside you. Here's what I know for sure:

- **If your idea persists beyond your objections, you must write this book.** The pain of hoarding ideas and never executing them is soul crushing. It's better to give things a try and see what happens than to always wonder if you could have written that book.
- **Your book doesn't have to look like others' books.** It doesn't have to be long and big. It just has to convey your message in your way and in your voice.
- **The process of writing your book has to suit you, your life and your needs.** Whatever you commit to has to ultimately be connected to you and why you care. Part of the job is learning how to trust yourself and commit to your process—because if it doesn't work for you, it doesn't work.
- **The work we do works us.** We become something more when we dedicate ourselves

to completing projects. Writing your book will transform you in ways you can't imagine now. The process of writing your book will help you develop your voice and your confidence. Your rewards will be profound and will empower your other projects.

⚡ **Writing a book takes time and it takes depth.** You will be called to write from your truth and your experience. You have been building up to this, and you are ready. Your efforts will be rewarded.

Believe it or not, you have plenty of wisdom and skills that you can apply to writing a book. I am here to help you structure your time, focus and energy so you can get your book done. You don't want to waste time, and you want to know where you are going with this. My intention is to help you:

◇ Quickly target your ideal reader.
◇ Clearly lay out the essentials that must be in your book.
◇ Develop a writing practice that works for you to get going.
◇ Navigate the challenges that will arise throughout the process.
◇ Finish your world-changing book!

I will ask you to adopt new perspectives that will serve your writing and build your confidence as an author. I will challenge you beyond what you think you can do because I believe you can write your book—if you stick with it. It's worth the time and effort.

Why do I care if you write your book or not? I have loved books for as long as I can remember. As a girl, I would bring home stacks of books from the library every week. I still do! Books have taken me places and introduced me to new ideas and people. The books I have written have changed lives, including my own. Books have inspired my imagination and grown me into the person I am today. I believe in the power of books to change the world, and I believe your book can change the world.

— How to use this book —

This book brings together everything I know from coaching writers since 1996. It offers a road map to help you design, enjoy and thrive in your own writing practice. You will then be able to write your book, and others, with joy and ease. The chapters are short and sweet. Reading them will be like having me as your coach on call. The tools and strategies in these pages will help anchor the writing process and guide you to make it your own. You should be able to pick up this book, find an answer to your question and get to writing. No long-winded stories or research. Just straight-talking support for you to get your words out, your way.

Consider this to be a workbook that will guide you through the writing process. You will be invited to do exercises like "free-writing" and to answer inquiries to help you clarify and focus your process and project. You will see these invitations throughout the book. Take what's useful for you. If it gets you writing, then it's useful. If you are trying something and writing isn't happening, discard that approach and explore something else.

This book is divided into five parts. Part one delves into the issues that most people face at some point in the book-writing process. Let's face it: much of the work of writing a book is battling with ourselves. We like to think it's just a matter of time, but in truth, the inner obstacles pose as much of a challenge as the outer obstacles. You can read part one all at once, or dip in as needed, like you would with a coach on call when problems arise to thwart your writing.

Part two gives a quick overview of how to get started writing your book. It's for the impatient author who wants to leap in now! Or perhaps you are a seasoned author but feel stuck with your new book. Part two will give you new approaches to become inspired by your writing again.

Part three addresses how to make time and space to write your book. It's where you will learn to set up a writing practice that you can consistently count on. You will begin to write in ways that work for you and your lifestyle.

Part four will help you organize your material. I cover what to write, how to organize the writing, how to structure the book and how to be sure your book is meeting your reader's needs.

Part five dives into the writing itself. I address the specifics on how to work through writing, revising and finishing the book. At the end, I provide a checklist of exercises and inquiries that have been shared throughout the book. The checklist can serve as a coaching home-work document, where you can easily see which activities you have completed and which need to be done. Feel free to jump around and use the exercises as you need them. Take what works for you, and then take action. It's time to write your world-changing book.

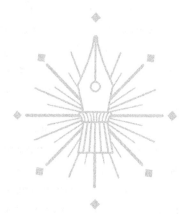

✑ *Part One* ✑

DEVELOP YOUR AUTHOR
MINDSET

"Mindset" is a trendy word these days—and for good reason. After many years of coaching, I know that the real game, the real place where change happens, is in our minds. At least half of my time spent with clients isn't talking about what they are doing with their writing but how they feel and think about it. The way we frame our projects drives how we experience the process. We face some deep stuff when we show up to speak our truth and put it in black and white.

When I was struggling with one of my books, my friend Carl pointed to my bookshelf. "Every one of those authors struggled too," he said. This stuck with me and helped me respect the work every author undertakes. **No one sidesteps the inner work of creating.** Navigating our fears and insecurities is required when we step up to put our ideas out there. But how great is that?! What better way to work through our "stuff" than through making stuff? **I believe our work grows us, and every challenging step is rewarded.**

Part one covers the issues that come up most frequently for my clients. I identify some of the common challenges that can sabotage any writer's success, and offer solutions to overcome them. When you encounter these speed bumps, this book will help you realize that they are a normal part of the writing process and not a reflection of your abilities or inadequacies. Read the whole section to prepare for obstacles, or dip in as needed.

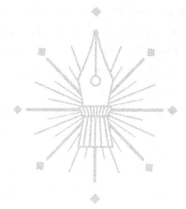

∽ WHY YOU MUST ∾
WRITE YOUR BOOK

Almost everyone doubts their legitimacy to write a book. Even when we are fired up, questions about our adequacy show up. A sneaky voice creeps out of our pillow around 3 a.m. and asks, "Who are you to write a book?" I will tell you who.

You are the person upon whom your great idea has landed. Like a brilliant bird circling, looking for a landing, your book idea has landed on you. And to continue the metaphor, it has roosted in your psyche for good. Elizabeth Gilbert talks about this in her book *Big Magic*. Your book is likely born from your work, or your experience. It's an expression of you and what you believe, know and do. **No one else could write this book that you have inside you.** This is the book you were meant to write. You may have never written a book or even thought of yourself as a writer. But your idea, process or story keeps asking—nay, *demanding* to be written. Don't worry if you aren't great at spelling or grammar. You can get help (a professional editor or Grammarly) to polish things up.

Perhaps you have told people about your idea and have gotten encouragement. Or you teach the content of your book, you see lives change as a result of your work, and you want that for more people.

In most cases, women feel a sense of rightness about their message—its clarity rings like a gong inside. Yet we also feel insecurity about it. Can we write it? How will we write it? Will anyone want to read it? Will it make the kind of difference we dearly hope it will?

What I have seen in my years as a writer's coach is that there comes a point where we simply need a nod from someone else. A "Yes! You can do this!" It's a kind of permission slip to do what we already deeply know to be right and true. *The Busy Woman's Guide* is that permission. It gives you the tools and approaches that will help you write your book in your way, your voice and your style.

Consider why you *must* write this book. Rather than try to logically validate why you are the person to write this book, tap into your heartfelt *why*. When you think of your book and the way it will change lives, it should move you. You will know when you hit upon your topic's core. It should move you, perhaps even to tears.

Use a Notebook to Contain Your Project

If you haven't already, create a container for this project. It could be a notebook or a digital file. Gather notes, drafts, ideas and images in one place for easy reference. It doesn't matter how messy the contents are, just that you have one container for your work. Ideally, it will be portable so you can access it everywhere. This is your book companion. I prefer to use a notebook, and one of my favorites is the Diary Flex by Hahnemühle, which is refillable.

You can also use the notebook as a progress log or way to capture your process. Sometimes we need to hash out our thoughts about our process or record information about our writing sessions—yay, gold star! Or add up our word count. We can log our ups and downs and have a record of what works and what doesn't for the next book we write.

Keep your author notebook with you as you read *The Busy Woman's Guide*. You can do the exercises and process your thoughts about your book in your notebook. Answering the questions I pose in one place will help you feel focused and organized.

EXERCISES

Get a container—a notebook or computer file—to capture all your ideas and inspiration for your book. No need to be fancy, just functional.

Write out your "why." Use the practice of free-writing, described more in part two, not to justify to the world or yourself why you are legitimate. Instead, free-write to clarify for *yourself* why you care enough to set aside the time and focus to get your ideas out of your head and into the world.

In your author notebook, write from the following prompt as a launching pad for your free-write: "I *must* write this book because . . ."

Set the timer for 15 minutes, put pen to paper or fingers to keyboard and *go*!

When the timer goes off, set your writing aside for a couple of hours or a day. Then read what you have written and extract one power sentence that sums up your "why" for writing this book. This sentence is your rallying cry. It will serve you when you lose your motivation, when fear tries to sideline you and when you just need something to get your butt in the writing chair.

Post your book's rallying cry where you will see it and gain strength and motivation from it. Print it up and hang it in your writing zone. Blaze it on the cover of your author notebook. Make it your screensaver on your phone or computer. Keep your "why" in front of you to inspire you to do the writing.

∽ WRITING A BOOK ∾
IS SOUL WORK

There's plenty of guidance out there about how to write a book. We are taught how to schedule our time, organize our material and pitch the idea to a publisher. There are classes and workshops devoted to writing books. But few people are talking about what it really takes to write a world-changing book: *soul*.

You have the smarts, and you have brought soul to your work. Now it's time to marry smart and soul together in a writing process that allows you to bring your ideas into form in ways that will resonate with your readers.

What do I mean by soul work? Soul work can be our life's work. Some people call this a sacred contract. Others think of it as a calling. It might not be your primary income or other work you get paid for, and it might not seem practical. Yet it's likely that your book is related to your profession or life experience in the same way *The Busy Woman's Guide* is an extension of decades of my helping people write. But just because it's right—and your soul work—doesn't mean it's not difficult. A teacher once told me that the soul is here to learn. I liked that. It made the challenges and obstacles I have faced feel like opportunities to grow rather than reasons to complain.

When I say that the work we do works us, this is what I am talking about. Your ego may have to take a side seat. You may have to ask for help. You will be asked to live with a lot of uncertainty. Your book will take longer and more from you than you think you have. It's a humbling process, for sure. I invite you to meet the challenges willingly.

When you know the meaning and purpose behind your book, you have arrived at your soul work. With this awareness rooted in your heart and soul, it will be easier to bring your mind and agenda along to make it happen. Your book is rising up to meet you. It persists in calling you out, and now is the time to accept the challenge of writing it.

What you give to your book will come back to you tenfold. You will gain confidence, self-knowledge, insights and power beyond what you have earned to date.

— INQUIRY —

What does soul work mean for you? Do you see your book as soul work?

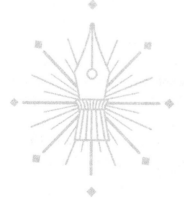

A Book Makes You a Conversation Leader

When I was promoting my novel, *Chasing Sylvia Beach*, I found a way to share the book's message that didn't feel like I was always shouting, "Buy my book!"

Instead, I paired two things that are important to me: life-changing conversations and leadership. I love rich conversations that bring out new ways of thinking and being. In my work as a coach, I get to talk with people about what's truly important to them. We dig deep to find the truth of their life and work and then seek ways to express that more on a daily basis. Leadership is also important to me. I believe that creative people and women are leaders. We have experiences that differ from the male experience. Now more than ever, we have the opportunity to initiate conversations to make the world a better place.

A book can serve as a conversation leader and an emissary, bringing your message to the world and leading the conversations you want to have. Women are being called to speak up and speak out like never before. Our voices and ideas are needed to help build a new way of being. And it's never been easier to write a book and get it out into the world. When you think about your book, return to your rallying cry.

Conversations and leadership matter to me. What matters to you?

At the core of your book are the things you care about deeply. Your book holds the key to the change you want to see in the world. There are many reasons to write a book, among them:

- To share your work with a larger audience.
- To claim your authority in your field so you can attract more opportunities.
- To tell the story that changed your life so it inspires others.

Each of these reasons is valid and may motivate you to write.

I found it helpful to have a reason connected to one of my core values—a reason that got me excited to do the work of writing and promoting, even when it felt scary. For me, it's about starting conversations, and a book is a conversation starter. My values of communication and life-changing conversations allowed me to think of the themes in my novel in a different way. When it came time to write articles and guest posts about my book, it was much easier to come from the place of initiating a discussion rather than marketing my book and trying to get someone to buy it.

Saying you are an author and sharing the content of your book leads to conversations that you want to have. **Our conversations can change the way we think, what we believe and how we act.** The world has plenty of problems that need solutions. They need you, a woman with something to say, to take the lead and offer your insights and expertise. Write your book. Lead the conversation.

EXERCISE

Make a list of the conversations that might spring up around the topics in your book. What do you want to be sure to talk about when discussing the book? These ideas can also be used as talking points when preparing for interviews about the book. Add to this list throughout the process of writing the book.

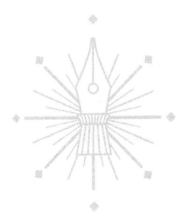

❧ YOUR BOOK WILL ❧
CHANGE THE WORLD

Most writers I encounter want their books to make a difference for others. They are on fire to share their wisdom, information and experiences because they want life and our world to be different.

Perhaps one person will read your book and think, feel and act differently because of it. Maybe hundreds or thousands of people will be inspired by your book.

I know for sure that finishing your book will change *your* world. Maybe it will help your business. Or it will be a calling card for your work, allowing you to do more of what you love. Perhaps writing a book is on your bucket list, something you have wanted to do forever—and finishing it will allow you to claim "author." To own it. However, you may be like many people who have trouble finishing things. Your inner critic *loves* this about you! It loves to keep your identity intact as someone who "never finishes things." Well, guess what? When you finish your book, that will no longer be true.

Ultimately, when we set out to write a book, we have no idea what will come of it. It's one of the biggest trust falls we will make. It can be easier to sacrifice the time and effort if we have a vision of what's possible when our book is finished.

I love helping women write world-changing books. My work with one person who writes a book has an exponential impact. This motivates me to get my work into the world even more.

EXERCISE

To help you get a sense of the gains waiting for you when you type "The End," think about the potential impact your book could have. First, take your time answering the following questions about the book's impact on you.

◇ What will be different for you when you
   finish your book?
◇ How do you hope this book will change your
   work and your life?
◇ What will change about your self-perception?
◇ What does the future look like when you have
   achieved your aim?

Now think about what you want for your reader. Imagine a bunch of your readers. They have read your book, loved it, implemented its teachings. Their lives have changed for the better. Answer these questions:

◇ What will change in your reader's life as a
   result of reading your book?

◇   How will your reader's life be better?

◇   How does your book impact your reader's communities, family and work?

— INQUIRY —

How will the world be different with your book in it? What do you imagine will change because of your book?

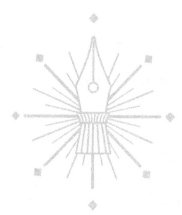

Seek a Publisher
or Self-Publish?

With more publishing options available today than ever before, it's important to decide before you start writing whether you will seek a publisher or self-publish. Each path will determine where you start. My advice may be the opposite advice you get from others. Whether you seek a publisher or publish your book on your own will depend on a number of things, including:

- Your goals for your book.
- Your "platform," meaning your ability to sell books to your audience.
- Your timeline and when you want your book to be out in the world.

Publishers are interested in how big your platform is. They want to know the extent of your influence, including social media networks and blogs. It's one thing to have thousands of people on your email list. It's another to have a list of people who will consistently buy what you are selling and who will rave about your book to all their friends. To seek a traditional publisher, you should already have a large, engaged audience. Publishers are risk-averse. They are looking for sure bets: celebrities and best-selling authors.

The time and energy it takes to build an engaged audience can take years. For most busy women, building a platform and writing a book at the same time is extremely difficult. To seek a publisher, you will need to find an agent to represent your book to editors at publishing houses—unless you prefer a small press or university press, some of which allow submissions directly from authors (see their websites for guidelines).

To attract the interest of an agent, you will need to write a compelling book proposal. A book proposal is a lengthy document used to sell a nonfiction book to a publisher. It's a sales document that builds a convincing argument for your book. I liken it to a graduate school application.

It can take months and much brainpower to pull together all the pieces for a proposal. The good thing about writing a book proposal is that it forces you to get extremely clear about the originality, clarity and salability of your book. You are going to have to do that no matter which path you choose. But if you self-publish, most of that work will go into the sales process when the book is done.

The majority of my clients prefer the more direct and empowering path of self-publishing. The truth is, publishers will spend very little time and energy helping you promote your book. So the promotion process will be up to you either way. Putting promotional thinking ahead of the book writing can dampen the energy for the book. Often we need to write it first to figure out what the book actually is. We need to glean the boons of writing the book and not waste precious time trying to sell the book to narrow-minded publishers.

"Hybrid" publishing offers a middle ground between traditional and self-publishing, where the author pays for certain services. Many companies offer this hybrid model to help authors publish on a more level playing field with traditional publishers. Some of these hybrid publishers include Inkshares and She Writes Press.

The benefits of self-publishing and hybrid publishing are extensive. You control the entire process from start to finish. You decide what, when and how you will publish. No publisher will make you change the title, the content or the cover of your book. You can launch the book in your own way and on your schedule. You can be innovative and do things that you might not be able to do with a publisher. And your piece of the financial pie is bigger, as royalties for self-publishing are better than royalties from a publisher. Companies like Ingram Spark, Lulu and Blurb make it easy to put together and distribute books.

Publishing fiction doesn't require a lengthy proposal but it does require other marketing materials, such as a synopsis. Typically, novelists finish a book, then seek a publisher. Nonfiction authors seek a publisher, then write the book when they have a contract.

You can probably tell which approach I prefer. After countless hours of pitching my novel to publishers, I realized that self-publishing was the path for me. Once I made this decision, I felt immediate relief and a sense of power. I wanted to control the timeline of its publication. I wanted to be responsible for the design of the book. I have self-published all of my books, and this is the path for me and most of my clients.

How will you decide? Answer the following questions to help you choose your book's path.

- **What's your timeline?** With a traditional publisher, it will take roughly eighteen months to bring the book to the shelves. If you do the project yourself, you control the timeline and can integrate the book into your business or work plans.

- **How are you with managing projects?** Being able to coordinate details, deadlines, manage your own time and focus are all part of the publishing job. If you work with a publisher or hybrid publisher, they will take the lead on details and deadlines. That doesn't mean you can turn everything over to them; you will be partially responsible for making decisions and executing your own marketing plans. How confident do you feel managing the details of a big project?

- **What's your funding plan?** If you self-publish, what's your budget? How will you fund your book? Even a low-cost approach can bring thousands of dollars in expenses for editing, design, and more. You may consider a crowdfunding campaign. That in itself is a major project, so consider carefully whether you have the bandwidth for that approach. You can do pre-sales on your own, which helps you gauge interest and generate revenue to fund the production costs. For traditional publishing, what costs are involved? It takes a lot of time to write a book proposal. You may hire help as I did to craft a solid pitch for a book I sought to publish.

- **How big is your influence?** Do you already have a large network or audience that will rally when you publish your book, buying copies for themselves as well as for gifts? Publishers want to see proof that you have an engaged audience (via social media, speaking gigs, other material you have written, etc.). You don't need a massive audience to self-publish.

- **What has worked for others?** Talk with authors who have written a similar kind of book to yours. Have a set of questions to keep things simple and concise. What surprised them? What would they do differently? What worked well?

Years ago, when I was building my writing competency, I didn't anticipate that the possibilities for publishing would be so vast and so in favor of authors. It has never been a better time to write a book—and on a scale that serves writers and our various agendas.

Hopefully this chapter has given you some ways to make a decision about which path to take. It's simply a brief overview to help you start thinking about your publishing options. An excellent resource to help educate you on publishing is *Green-Light Your Book* by Brooke Warner.

Wherever you are on the publishing timeline, at some point you will have to write your book. This book is focused on how to get your book out onto the page.

EXERCISE

Free-write to get to the heart of which publishing path feels right for you. Then list three reasons why you chose this path. If needed, talk with a trusted friend or advisor. This is a big and personal decision that has to feel right for you.

~ CHOOSE ~
WHICH BOOK TO WRITE FIRST

You may have more than one book in you. If so, choosing which one to write first can be challenging. This choice is something you will have to decide for yourself based on a number of factors:

- Your hopes/dreams for monetizing your book.
- The type of book you are writing and its length.
- How your book fits into your business or career goals.
- Whether an agent or publisher has expressed interest in your book.
- Your gut feeling, or instinct, about which book you want to write first.

Do a free-write to get deeper into the answer about which book you should write first. You will notice that throughout this book, I suggest free-writing as a way to get clarity for yourself. It's amazing how much more insight can come through free-writing as opposed to just thinking or talking through the issues.

There are many types of books you can write. Books related to your work and how-to books are the kinds of book I refer to most in this book. But personal essays and memoirs will also benefit from the ideas I present.

If you are writing a book of personal stories, consider digging a little deeper when it comes to the chapter "Identify Your Reader" in part four. The issues your book addresses might be more philosophical and personal-growth oriented, thereby having the potential to inspire or motivate a reader.

Your book might be a blend of your own stories and some guidance. In her book *Soulful Simplicity*, Courtney Carver shares both her personal journey and specific guidance on how we can simplify our lives for more satisfaction. Her tagline and Instagram account are called "Be More with Less," and that's the basic promise of her book. We all want to be more, right? But how to do it with less stuff and less activity, that's new.

In *Your Story Is Your Power* by Elle Luna and Susie Herrick, the authors help the reader excavate their stories and live in new, empowering ways as a result of knowing and owning their stories. The exercises in the book are fabulous, and the stories the authors tell to accompany the exercises help make them sticky. While the book isn't personal essays or memoirs per se, a little bit of this kind of writing blended throughout makes the book more powerful. The colorful illustrations add a lot to the book as well.

Fiction writers, if you are writing a novel or short stories, *The Busy Woman's Guide* may not be the best book for you. Elements of plot, characters, setting and other aspects of fiction aren't addressed here. I suggest

Donald Maass's book *Writing the Breakout Novel* and its accompanying workbook for guidance with fiction. Another excellent fiction-writing guide is *The Writer's Journey* by Christopher Vogler.

It may take time to choose which book is first. This is something only you can decide. Use your intuition and your instincts alongside your intellect to choose.

— INQUIRY —

What book will you start with, and what makes that a good choice for you?

❧ Commit to a ❧
Monogamous Relationship
with Your Book

While it might be appealing to dream of going away to a writing retreat for a week or weekend, the reality is that you will probably write most of your book in the interstices of your life. But because you don't want "Write book" to be something on your calendar that you see and dread, you will want to find ways to integrate it into your life so it's easy to drop into and get your words out on the page.

Consider that writing a book is a new relationship you are entering into. The book is a place where you connect with your ideas and yourself. It's a repository of your ideas and what you want for the world.

As women, we tend to be relationship focused, so let's make that work for you and your book. **Instead of thinking of your book as something that takes time away from your current relationships, consider it a new and exciting relationship that you get to devote time and attention to.**

Consider your author self. She's super smart but not intimidating. She's the kind of person you want to be with because she always has something to say. Most of the time it's good stuff too, insights and observations that somehow bring light to your life. She has a way with words, that one!

She's a great friend and is always there when you want to connect. You can tell her anything. She can take it. She's wise and because she knows you well, she can help you shift into new ways of thinking, being and acting. She's that kind of friend who makes you feel like a better version of yourself just by spending time with her. How cool is that? You will love getting to know your author self.

Clients ask me if they can work on a book and another project at the same time. Maybe two books are vying for your attention. It's easy to think we can spread our creative love around. Everyone has to discover this for themselves, and in my experience, it's very hard to do our day-to-day roles and juggle two major projects at once. Every project we have going is like a burner on our stove cooking away. It may be on low, it may be on high, but it's taking away from our ability to focus. It may not seem detrimental, but losing our precious focus because of many projects can really slow us down.

If you have a record of being able to drive multiple projects consistently over the finish line with your sanity intact, by all means go right ahead. But I suggest becoming a creative serial monogamist, finishing one project at a time so you can give each its due. Keep a file or notebook for all your other projects. Use the magic phrase "for now." For now, I'm focusing on my book. For now, I'm setting aside other projects. For now, I'm in a monogamous relationship with my book.

Take good care of this relationship. Follow through with all the dates you set aside to write your book. The power of keeping those promises to yourself cannot be overstated. The more you show up for your book, the easier it will become to devote time to it. If you find yourself avoiding your book, ask yourself what it will take to get back in touch with it. You can always do a free-write about the current state of your relationship with your book.

— INQUIRY —

What does a healthy relationship with your book and author self look like on your busiest week?

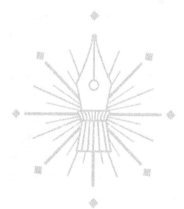

LACK OF TIME IS YOUR BEST FAKE EXCUSE

The most common excuse people give for not doing their creative work is a lack of time. Is that you clinging to this tired excuse? I know how valid this excuse seems. Everyone nods and commiserates because we are all victims of the ticking clock and our propensity to overfill our time with activities. It's all too easy to use this excuse as a crutch for deferring our writing dream. But I have coached everyone from extremely busy executives to retirees to working mothers, and here's the truth: we make time for what's important to us.

How do we shift from the cultural paradigm of "busy" to believing and acting on the notion that we give time to things that matter to us? Here are some strategies that my clients have used to go from excuse maker to author:

- **Get emotion savvy.** Notice the thoughts or feelings that arise when you consider writing. Your fears and insecurities are usually what's in the way, not lack of time.
- **Get real.** Disengage from the notion that you don't have time to do what matters to you. Be a heroine, not a victim, of your creative impulses.

- **Get clear.** Return to your rallying cry for writing your book. This is your stake, your driving motivation. If you don't know this in one gut-vibrating sentence, you will easily blow off your writing sessions for laundry, dates with friends, shopping, whatever.

- **Get focused.** When writing a book, some things need to fall away temporarily. To be a creator, consider reducing your consumption. No need to become a hermit; just reduce the amount of time you spend consuming news, scrolling social media feeds and watching TV or movies.

- **Get balanced.** As we spend more time bouncing around online, it gets harder to quiet ourselves and focus on the deeper work of writing. Distinguish between two kinds of attention: (1) fragmented and "out there" and (2) focused on your topic. Balance time between the two. It's not always easy to step away from the bustle to go into the writing cave, but it's always, always satisfying.

- **Get support.** We tend to honor our commitment to others more than our own self-commitments. Honestly, accountability is one of the main reasons people hire a coach to help them write their books. It's not that I have such brilliant advice—it's all pretty simple, as you can see. We value what we pay for, and if we pay someone to help us, we are going to rise to the occasion to get our money's worth.

What do you notice about your relationship with time and your book? What do you hear yourself saying and thinking about time or lack of it?

Why It's So Hard to Focus

As I write this, I am sitting in a café next to an acquaintance. I know she wants to write a book. When we both sat down, we each said we were here to write. My fingers have been flying on the keyboard. Hers haven't. They have been tickling her phone because every couple of minutes, someone pings her and she picks up the phone to respond. If my phone has been pinging, I wouldn't know it—it's in my purse, and with the loud café music, it's out of range of my hearing.

The time I have spent here today has been a rare and precious period of focus, and my computer battery is going to run out soon. I am more invested in leaving here feeling *good* from having gotten my desired writing done than in responding to others' agendas.

Maintaining focus is an ever-greater challenge as we live a more connected lifestyle, checking our social media feeds, scanning the internet for yet more stimulus. But if you are trying to write a book or create on a regular basis, you must learn to command a certain level of focus. The minute you leave your project and go off on another thread, it's as if you have put yourself back at the beginning. You have taken one step forward and two steps back.

We don't have to be available 24/7. As women, we are oriented toward making sure everyone else and everything else is taken care of before we do our own work. These days it's incredibly hard to find the focus required to write anything, let alone a book. Yet we must cultivate our ability to focus. A special kind of attention is required to say what we want and need to say.

Assess how much focus you have for all the projects and obligations in your life. You can have a lot on your plate and still be able to focus. *Everyone talks about time management, but what's really required for your creative work is focus management.*

Harnessing your focus is like shutting the door to your office or writing room. You are temporarily holding off your other obligations to dive into your own work. Consider how easily you move between tasks, roles and projects. Are you able to release your thoughts about other obligations and drop into a focused state?

I hope that you learn to love the focus you have when writing, that you can drop into a zone where you are in touch with both your material and how you want to communicate it. This will require some training. Consider that the real work of writing a book is less about time management and more about focus management. *The quality of your focus will determine the quality of your writing and your book.*

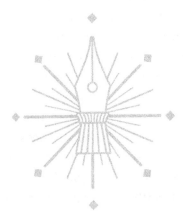

ᴅᴏ Yᴏᴜ Hᴀᴠᴇ
Sᴘᴀᴄᴇ ᴛᴏ Wʀɪᴛᴇ ᴀ Bᴏᴏᴋ Nᴏᴡ?

We have tackled the time monster. Now let's look at the space required to write a book.

Most of us juggle many priorities: children, work, home, significant other and more. It's not easy to find space or bandwidth. In addition, we underestimate how much space things take, and I am not just talking about physical space. There's also mental, physical and temporal space.

You know that feeling when you finish something? You feel space open up. Like putting away the holiday decorations, completing a project at work or finishing a school year. You have time and energy to bring something else onto your plate. You also know the feeling of overwhelm, having too many things to manage.

When my clients come to me feeling overwhelmed, I ask them to identify their tipping point. When is it all too much?

What obligations on *your* plate put you over the edge? Hopefully, with awareness, you can learn to stop committing before you are plunged into overwhelm.

I have had clients who added book writing to their agenda in the same year that they were either buying a new house, moving to a new country, moving parents out of a childhood home, getting a new job or moving across the country. Guess what happened to their books? They aren't on the shelves of bookstores. They are sitting in computer files waiting for actual space and the commitment to be written. No amount of coaching could reduce the amount of space those other things were taking in my clients' lives. It just wasn't the right timing for them to write their book.

You have a full life too. You are busy. But that doesn't mean you can't make space to write your world-changing book. You may have heard of the "write your book in a weekend" workshops. The truth is, it's going to take much longer than that to get your book written and into a form that's ready to share with the world. Like renovation projects, your book will take longer and require more from you than you might expect.

The biggest mistake people make when getting ready to add a book to their plate isn't removing obligations. Sometimes when I ask clients what they will put on hold, they stubbornly say, "Nothing!"

We have a skewed perception of how much we can actually do at any given time. The space in our imagination is vast—infinite, even. Yet the space we have in a day is, alas, limited. Our energy isn't always full steam either. So we have to go with the flow of what's manageable in any given week. We need to make space on our calendar for writing time, organizing, researching and all the other tasks associated with writing a book. Some things will contribute directly to our book. Clients, teaching, interacting with our book's audience, networking at conferences. There may be volunteer obligations or other family obligations to set aside while writing the book.

Now, I am the last person to use the word "realistic." I learned early on from a former yo-yo pro boyfriend (that's right, *yo-yo pro*) that anything is possible—and I have seen all kinds of "unrealistic" things happen in my clients' lives. I believe the word "realistic" exists largely to shut down innovation and creativity. But in assessing whether you have the space to write a book, you do want to bring in a dose of realism. The last thing I want for you is to add another stressor into your life. It's okay if now isn't the time to write your book. Setting yourself up with the space to succeed will build competence and confidence that will allow you to enjoy writing the book.

EXERCISE

Let's take a look at your current commitments. Here's an exercise my clients have found useful to see what they are committed to. I call it "Mind-Mapping Your Plate," based on the common phrase "so much on my plate." Putting your obligations visually on one page can give an immediate sense of how much you are actually taking on.

Get a regular sheet of printer paper. **On sticky notes or in drawn bubbles, jot down all the major projects and commitments you have over the next three months.** They could include:

◇ Your day job or business (and number of hours/week).
◇ Special projects at work, like a promotion or a launch.
◇ Buying a home.
◇ Moving to another home, state or country.
◇ Parenting responsibilities, like kids' extracurricular activities or sports events.
◇ Volunteer work.
◇ Travel plans.
◇ Social and recreational activities.
◇ Family obligations, like parents' or siblings' moves or other caretaking responsibilities.
◇ Household projects, such as renovating or gardening.

When you see all your current commitments on the page, it's easy to get a true picture of your availability. This is where you may see what you can set aside while you write your book. As you go through your months writing, many opportunities will arise. How will you fend off more projects and keep your writing space intact? Sometimes we have to spell it out for ourselves. I once made a sign that says "Add No More." When I pull it out and hang it in my writing space, it reminds me not to add more things to my plate.

Perhaps you thought that because of the title of this book, I would have a magic solution to help you write your book even when you are juggling other major projects. Yes, I can help you, *and* you will have to make time, space and focus for your book. Consider if this is the right time for you to take on another project.

— INQUIRY —

Are you able and willing to commit space to making your book a priority?

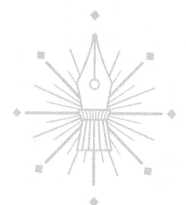

❧ Befriend Your ❧
Inner Critic and
Transform Resistance

Nothing brings out the inner critic like committing to writing a book. When you take action toward your dreams, your fears and your inner critic will grow and try to overwhelm your dedication. This is normal, so don't take extra inner critic activity as a sign that you should stop writing and clean the basement instead. At some point in the writing process, you will feel blocked by this internal voice. Don't worry. Once you understand how it works in your creative world, it will be easier to overcome resistance.

Exercise

Here's my method I give to my clients to help them free themselves of the grip of the inner critic. They have called it life changing. Do this process now to have an advance defense against your inner meany. Or use this as an emergency exercise when you feel paralyzed by fear and insecurities. Don't skip the writing part; it will reveal insights that will help you stay on track.

1. **Pay your inner critic the attention it craves.** Hear it as a distinct voice. Notice its tone. What does it say? What are some of its favorite expressions?

2. **Describe your inner critic.** Set a timer for 15 minutes and do a free-write character sketch of your inner critic. Explore what it looks like, where it lives, what it eats. What's its name? What does it wear? Get a clear picture of it as distinct from you.

3. **Set boundaries with your inner critic.** Once you have identified your inner critic, you can design a relationship with it that allows you to do your writing. Send it to the office supply store while you write. Tell it you will listen to it two days after your writing session but not a moment sooner. What boundaries do you want to establish when it tries to sabotage your writing? Be kind but firm.

4. **Keep your sense of humor.** When your inner critic shows up, stay light. The inner critic has heavy messages, and using humor and lightness is another way not to subscribe to the bad news it wants you to believe. Thank the inner critic. Thank it for its input, and keep going.

5. **Enroll the inner critic's help.** If your inner critic hounds you about your terrible spelling skills, ask it how it can help improve them. Know that everyone has an inner critic, and millions of books have been written in spite of it.

6. **Finally, engage in a written dialogue.** Ask and answer these important questions in writing: What does your inner critic want for you? How can it help you? What's its new role on your book-writing team? Then commit to developing a conscious and healthy relationship with your inner critic instead of letting it squelch your dreams.

--- INQUIRY ---

What has shifted for you as a result of getting to know your inner critic?

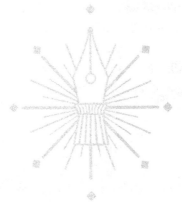

ALIGN WITH YOUR INNER CHAMPION

We are quite familiar with our inner critic. But we also have an inner champion who can help us past the speed bumps in the writing process. We may start off whining or dumping our fears and complaints onto the page. It's as if the inner critic holds the pen. But within minutes, another voice emerges. An encouraging voice. A kind voice. It's the part of us that knows we must try, and it gives us courage to write and risk other creative challenges. This reassuring side of us is usually drowned out by the inner critic. But when we write, our inner champion somehow seems to show up more readily with support.

You may already have seen glimpses of your inner champion. Who is this part of you? Let's get to know this encouraging force so you can access it anytime.

EXERCISE

Use a free-write to invite a stronger connection to your inner champion. Have fun discovering more about this part of you that knows you can do it. Answer these questions in your author notebook:

◇ What encouraging words or phrases does your inner champion have for you?

◇ Does your inner champion have a name?

◇ What does your inner champion look like?

◇ What does your inner champion love about you?

◇ What does an ongoing relationship with your inner ally look like?

Often when I am struggling with a problem, I jot it down in a paragraph or two. Then I ask my inner champion for advice. This may sound odd, but turning the problem over to the pen always yields wisdom I wouldn't have accessed through thinking. This has been helpful in life and for my writing.

— INQUIRY —

How can your inner champion help motivate you?

⬲ RELEASE GUILT ⬳
ABOUT TAKING TIME FROM
OTHER OBLIGATIONS

Some people say writing a book is the hardest thing they have ever done. One surprising challenge we face when taking time for our own projects is feeling guilty. When we play many roles, we can feel pulled between them. It seems like the things we love compete for our time. **When we put our commitments in competition against each other, we set ourselves up to lose.** We want to feel like our life and work are integrated. When we make space for the things we are committed to, we don't have to fight them.

Writing your book will demand a lot from you. Yet the guilt you feel when you take time to write will only detract from your ability to enjoy your work and your life. This guilt is optional. It's not serving any purpose other than to degrade your daily satisfaction with your life.

Be present with the roles you inhabit at any given time. Don't write during the times you know you like to be with your children. Don't steal important spouse time to write your book. This might mean scheduling a new time when you can write, such as a 15-minute session every day instead of hours of uninterrupted writing time.

Guilt will try to creep in. Don't let it. What can you replace it with? Perhaps a sense of devotion. The strength of commitment. The humility you experience when faced with the work required. Love for your subject can pull you through. A desire for the world to be different as a result of your book. Remember your rallying cry.

— INQUIRY —

How can you set up your book writing so you don't feel guilty taking time from your other obligations? What will help you deflect any guilt that arises when you take time to work on your book?

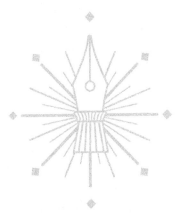

⟲ Rally Your Allies ⟳

One way to help deal with possible "competition" for your book time is to rally your allies. This includes letting your loved ones know the importance of your book commitment. Otherwise, they may see you slipping away from them and feel distance instead of connection.

There comes a time when talking with our people about the significance of our writing is *vital*. But we are rarely proactive about it. I get it. Sometimes the people closest to us don't understand our dreams.

No one knows how important your writing is except you. There are as many ways to get support as there are different kinds of people who can share the process of writing your book. Be thoughtful about who is in on your writing process. Here are five types of people you might consider your writing allies.

— Peers —

These are your fellow writers, the people in your writing classes or your writing buddies. Even if they aren't writing in the same genre, style or subject matter, your peers can provide:

- Feedback on your chapters.
- A sounding board for your process.
- A forum to share resources for developing your craft and publishing your work.
- Accountability partners to help you stay on track.

Most importantly, peer relationships help you feel "gotten." Being understood is crucial to writers and artists who are creating something from nothing. My peer relationships helped me and made the writing journey much more pleasant. The friendships I developed at La Muse writing retreat in France and the writing buddy-ships I had in Boulder with Suzanne, Ann and Dorothy were all invaluable to my novel.

MENTORS AND TEACHERS

Writing instructors, mentors and professional editors deeply understand the craft of writing, and some have written books themselves. They will be able to assess your work as a whole and offer critical and constructive insights.

After an initial novel writing workshop in 1999, I relied on professional editors to guide my work. Hiring a developmental editor to critique my manuscript was for me like taking a master class in novel writing. I did this at least four times in 12 years and it was well worth the investment.

— AUDIENCE MEMBERS —

These people won't necessarily offer a critical review of your work. Instead, they will respond as someone who would ultimately buy and read your book—in other words, the person you are writing for. Once you have established your core message and content, it can be helpful to pass it by your ideal reader.

Three "beta" readers volunteered to read an early draft of this book. I wanted to make sure I was on the right track and also to see if anything was missing. I polished my draft as well as I could before giving it to them.

Each beta reader confirmed that my timeline would work for them. I clarified what I needed—and what I didn't need—and made it easy for them to give feedback by sharing my file in Google Docs. Their feedback was priceless, and I thanked them with a choice of a gift card or a coaching session.

Before you hand your book over to readers, do at least two drafts to ensure it's as good as you can make it. Ask specific questions to get the best feedback, including which chapters resonate most, which lose their interest, what's missing and what might be too much. Be open to their feedback. (For more guidance in soliciting feedback, see "Design the Feedback Process" in part five.)

— FRIENDS AND FAMILY —

Your people love you, but they may not "get" your work. They have a certain perspective of you and perhaps a hidden or obvious agenda. They may not resonate with your book's message and, therefore, are usually not the best source for objective feedback. However, if you don't let your family and friends in on your work, they may become another obstacle on your writing path. Design agreements with them about the boundaries you need. You don't have to go into the details of what you are writing, but you do want to let them know what you need. Be specific. Ask for the time, space and respect you need to pursue your writing. Tell them about your dedication to your book and why that's important to you now. You may want to make a "Writing: Do Not Disturb" sign to hang on your door. You may ask for extra help around the home.

Consider telling your friends that, for now, you aren't as available as you used to be. Again, be specific; let them know that your mornings are for the book. Or that Thursday evening is your writing date with yourself. You may even have a friend who is also writing a book and can be your accountability buddy.

— SOCIAL MEDIA BUDDIES —

Sometimes our social media networks can serve much like writing buddies. Making a public announcement about your book is one form of public accountability. You can share your process, celebrate your milestones and use your postings as a sort of online journal. Some people get a lot of value and support from making a public announcement on social media. Others need to have a strong privacy cocoon around their project.

When you finally reach the end of your book, it will be clear how much the acknowledgments page truly reflects the support you received along the way. Many people will have contributed. But if you don't line up your allies, you risk having those important people becoming detractors and saboteurs, hindering your ability to write your book.

EXERCISE

Make a list of who your allies will be. Next, write down your requests for time, space and support. Then, when you are ready, meet with these people and make clear your requests so you can enjoy having support for writing your book.

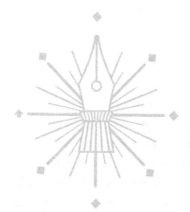

DEFLECT YOUR
DETRACTORS

Along with your allies, there also, sadly, will be people whose thoughts and opinions are less than helpful. People have all kinds of reactions to someone writing a book. You have probably already experienced a range of responses to your enthusiastic declaration, "I'm writing a book!" Envy, competition for your time, a change of status and power, and fear of losing you altogether may play a part in someone being a detractor when you wish they would be a supporter. Even our closest people can become adversaries of the book.

In the prior chapter, we looked at the importance of determining who you will let in on your book project. Similarly, it's wise to decide who you don't need to share much with—the people who just don't need to be privy to your writing process. Being asked, "How's the book going?" can be a well-meaning question that actually doesn't help.

Writing a book can be a very private thing, and it takes much longer than most people expect. Having to constantly report to friends and family about its progress can be draining. Sometimes, saying we are writing a book becomes too much. The "b" word (book) can become too weighty, even in our own minds. And I have seen that **the more we talk about writing, the less we are doing it.** Remember to establish the boundaries that work best for you. I recommend letting your "inner circle" know—your family, best friends and coach or mentor. Then keep your head down and focus on writing the book, not talking about it.

EXERCISE

Make a list of people you won't be sharing much with during the book-writing process and the boundaries you will establish. Keep this private; this process is just for you.

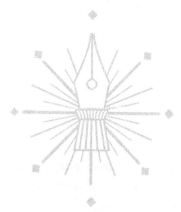

⌒ SUDDENLY AND ⌒
FREQUENTLY STRUCK CLUELESS

The idea for your book seemed so clear. You grabbed the inspiration, made a rough outline and dove into scribbling your ideas down. Soon enough, your enthusiasm burbled over into chaos. You lost the thread of logic and now your writing just feels like a handful of messy incoherence. Take heart. You may experience any or all of the following signs of cluelessness while writing your book:

- You doubt you have any authority about what you are saying.
- You are a blank slate when it comes to knowing how to structure your material.
- You wonder if your concepts make sense to anyone but you and your cats.
- You fret that you are completely unoriginal and your book has already been done by someone else.
- You cringe at the thought of others' judgment of your book.
- You are certain your book will prove you to be a total nincompoop.
- You dread the daunting publishing "adventure."

Right, then. Much better to go back to the laundry and the very demanding business of our lives. Isn't it much easier to avoid all this cluelessness? **Authors make a choice again and again along the path of writing a book: stay safe or risk the unknown repercussions of sticking our neck and ideas out there.**

I have written three books and five e-books. I have helped hundreds of writers find their footing on their writing paths. Based on these experiences, I believe that if we have the impulse to write or create something, it's our duty to follow that impulse—and I believe it's totally worth it.

For all the terrifying uncertainty inherent in the creative process, here's what will make the "it" all worth it for you:

◇ You will feel wildly exuberant when you write from your wisdom and authenticity.
◇ You will vibrate with your truth for hours after writing it.
◇ You will feel more connected to your vitality and to your unique essence after writing.
◇ This vitality will ripple out to the rest of your life, energizing your people, your work and even strangers.
◇ You will respect yourself more after writing.

But don't take my word for it. Stick it out at the page or keyboard and feel the results yourself. Pay attention to what you gain from writing your book consistently. When these and other fears rise up to convince you that you don't have any authority to put your words on paper, know that wrangling them is one of the most fun, sweatiest and rewarding parts of claiming your authorship. Hang in there through the cluelessness and trust that your book is on the other side—if you stick with it.

— INQUIRY —

What will help you navigate those moments of cluelessness? Don't forget a healthy sense of humor.

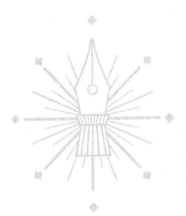

⟫ Glean the Immediate ⟪ Benefits of Writing

Writing your book will require time, focus, attention, humility and courage. But your project will also give back. And not just when it's finished. Throughout the process, you will slowly and subtly gain confidence. You will fall in love with your material all over again. You will enjoy how it feels to really know and share your expertise in this new way.

I believe that our creativity is the source of our vitality. When we are creating, we are tapping into our truest aliveness. We ignite our life energy when we create. We generate new energy. This energy feels so much better than the dread or pain of avoiding our writing. Quite frankly, this is the primary reason I coach authors. **I want everyone to enjoy the aliveness that we generate when we are doing our creative work.**

Now, here's the weird thing. Usually, you won't "feel" like writing. Your mind will trick you into thinking everything else is more important. That's why **we build structures around our writing so we don't get lost in feelings or insecurities.** We build a writing practice that helps us cross the river of resistance.

What if you had a reflection process that allowed you to feel the benefits of writing throughout the whole process? Simple, quick, but potent, capturing the vibe of the sessions will help you notice and savor more. The cool thing is you will begin to appreciate that working on your book is *working you.* You are writing this for others, but doing the work is having a positive impact on you. The first world you are changing is your own.

Exercise

Here's a simple practice to help you notice the difference your writing is making in your life on a regular basis. At the end of each writing session, in your author notebook, jot down three words that describe how the writing session was for you. Don't overthink this; just write three words that reflect your experience. You will certainly see a range of experiences on your list. Some days might be "slogging, hard, good" or "freeing, fun, challenging." Keep a running list to witness how the writing is changing you.

∾ *Part Two* ∾

GET STARTED WRITING

This book is written for busy women. You don't have time for fluff. You want to know what to do, how to do it and when.

Part two provides a quick guide with five steps to get you started:

1. Make free-writing your power tool.
2. Use the timer to stay focused.
3. Gather your project-based writing prompts.
4. Write in short bursts using your prompts.
5. Schedule your writing time.

The sooner you start writing, the sooner you will build confidence, get material out of your head and get into the practice of writing. This is a competency—the ability to write your ideas—that you will use time and again. You may not feel like you have a grip on what the book will look like, much less have an outline. That's okay. You are going to have to practice writing in any case, so get started now.

In *Bird by Bird*, Anne Lamott talks about writing a shitty first draft. When we create a complete—albeit crappy—first draft, we gain confidence. We now have material we can work with instead of just a bunch of ideas. I like calling it the shaggy first draft. Following the five steps in this section will help you write your shaggy first draft.

MAKE FREE-WRITING YOUR POWER TOOL

Free-writing is the key to making writing easy. Popularized by Natalie Goldberg in her 1986 book *Writing Down the Bones*, this method enables you to get your words onto paper while getting past fears and overanalyzing. I swear by this method. I wrote my novel and all my books, articles and blogs using the free-write method and have taught it to hundreds of writers.

For those unfamiliar with free-writing, you simply write for a short period of time without stopping. You don't worry about coherence, precision, propriety or getting anything correct. The point is to just spill your thoughts onto the paper—without judgment. You can revise later, I promise.

One obstacle most of us face when writing a book is thinking that the first draft is the last draft. I am sorry to bring the news to you, but you will do several drafts. I don't tell you this to discourage you but to help you realize that your perfectionist self doesn't need to be on the job for the first round. The shaggy first draft is just getting your ideas out onto the page so you can organize and refine them later.

Free-writing works so well because when we write quickly and without censorship, we move past the controlling mind that tries to stop us. You know the voices: *"Don't say that." "That's not nice." "You can't tell that!"* We all have them, and those voices can stop us before we even get started. With free-writing, we can zoom right past them. What a relief to have permission to write without being overly concerned about quality on the first round!

The next chapter offers a simple tool to make free-writing easy. For a more in-depth guide to free-writing, go to the chapter "Free-Write Your Shaggy First Draft" in part five.

EXERCISE

Try a quick free-write now. Set a timer for 10 minutes. Use the prompt "I write because . . ."

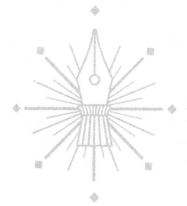

USE A TIMER TO
STAY FOCUSED

A timer is one of the most powerful tools for writing. The unrestrained nature of the free-write partners with the timer to keep your hand moving, to keep the censor at bay and to provide the glue to keep your butt in the chair while you write. You can also use the timer to track how much you are writing each week. Some of my clients like to tally writing hours so they can see how much progress they are making.

Don't underestimate the power of the timer. You may already have figured out that it's the simplest things in life that are the most effective. The timer is one of them. If your writing could use a power boost, the timer will lead the way to fuller expression.

Many of my clients use their phone. Others like the meditation app Insight Timer for their writing. You can program interval bells to signify warm-up writing periods. The timer will hold your focus and allow you to get your words out in your own voice. Sometimes, the timer urges us to speed up. If you find yourself racing to get your words out, take a deep breath and remind yourself that you can take as much time as you need. No rush. Just focus.

EXERCISE

Choose a timer that works for you. Experiment with 5-, 10- and 15-minute free-writing sessions. Set the timer and then dive into a free-write. Build up your writing stride over time.

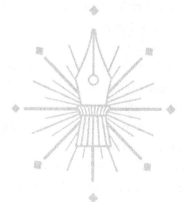

GATHER YOUR
PROJECT-BASED
WRITING PROMPTS

Before you launch into a free-write, you may be wondering, *But what do I write about?* Isn't it odd that when we commit to writing, our great ideas seem to evaporate?

If you are like all the other writers I know, you are a fount of endless possibilities. Where are all those ideas when you are ready to write about them? They are still in there. You just need to pin them down. Here's how:

- **Start a list of things you want to include in your book.** Keep them in one place: a digital document in Evernote, Word, Google Docs or in your notebook. Put 50 things on the list. That's right—50. Trust me, you will have at least that many.
- **List anything that seems relevant to your book's topic.** At this point, no item is too small or insignificant. Anecdotes, stories, theories, ideas, research to follow up on, put it all down. Don't censor yourself or worry about

being methodical or tidy yet. Add to the list over time.

- ❧ **Keep your prompt list with you.** You want to be able to quickly add ideas to the list, so capture your ideas in one place. Don't use the random-slips-of-paper method of organizing. Once you start collecting ideas to write about, your mind will feed you more and more. It's fun. If you see patterns, gather the prompts into categories. This will help you when it's time to generate a table of contents. Your list will become a loose and wild table of contents that you can write from.

- ❧ **Use your prompts as the diving board for your free-writes.** Start working your way down the list in order. Or write the prompts on index cards and pick one at random to write from. You can post the cards on a wall or corkboard to see all your ideas at once. Or you can put them in a bowl or basket and pull them at random. Over time, you will accumulate writing that you can revise and hone into complete pieces. But first, just free-write. Go through every prompt and write even the shaggiest draft of what you want to say. Don't worry about perfection; that will come later.

Getting all your ideas out like this may feel overwhelming. There's so much to say! How will you organize it all? One of the biggest fears we face when writing a book is that our free-writing time will be unfocused, unproductive and, worse yet, a waste of time. But trust me, you will write your way to clarity. These prompts are simply guideposts to get you started. In part four of this book, I will help you organize your book's content.

Exercise

Start getting your ideas on paper by gathering your writing prompts. Choose your capture system and make it work for you.

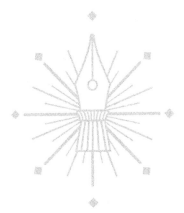

WRITE IN SHORT BURSTS
USING YOUR PROMPTS

Fifteen minutes per day—that's all you need to get started on your book. Chances are, once you set the timer for 15 minutes and begin to write, you won't want to stop. Great! Keep going. Set the timer for another 15 minutes, then another.

Everyone, no matter how busy they are, has these small windows of time into which they can squeeze some writing. One of the biggest misconceptions new writers have is thinking they need big chunks of time to write.

You may think you need a whole day, or a half day, or a weekend in a cabin alone. But then it never happens because even a two-hour period is hard to schedule. Perhaps you have read about a well-published author who writes for several hours each day. You might assume that you too, should write all morning, or all afternoon, or all day, even.

When you begin a new skill, you take small steps. If you were going to learn piano, you wouldn't start with a Beethoven sonata. You would start with scales. You just need brief chunks of time, say, 15 minutes per day. Brief writing sessions are akin to scales for musicians. Practice, practice, practice. Soon you will be writing for hours.

I heard about a woman who wrote a novel in five minutes a day. Yup, five. Imagine what you could do in 15 minutes! I can usually do two 40-minute sessions of focused writing in a two-hour period. And that's on the good days. That's plenty. One or two of those sessions per week really add up. Start small and build. Don't set yourself up to fail by thinking you need an hour to write. You will work up to that.

EXERCISE

This week, write from at least two of your prompts. Use the three-word reflection process (see the exercise in "Glean the Immediate Benefits of Writing" in part one) to see how it feels for you to get started writing.

SCHEDULE YOUR WRITING TIME

Make it easier on yourself by scheduling time for writing. Tuck the writing time into your lunch hour or into your morning before everyone wakes up. Write at the park, a café or the library on your way home from work. Sit in the car before you go into work and scribble for 15 minutes. If you take public transportation, write on the train or bus. You can fit it in anywhere.

At the beginning of each week, schedule your writing time. Put it into your calendar. My clients say that once it's in the schedule, it happens. So put it in the schedule. You may have heard the advice to write at the same time every day. If you can manage to slot the same time in every day, that's excellent. If not, catch your writing time where you can.

It's best not to plan writing at the end of the day. People who try to write before (or in) bed have reported that it's much more difficult, the writing isn't focused and it becomes a chore they dread. **Write earlier in the day and the energy you get from writing will fuel the rest of your day.** If possible, schedule your writing slot for when you will have extra time after your regular 15-minute session. You may get on a roll and want to keep going!

That's it! With the five steps presented in this section, you will be able to get started writing. Read on to access ways to navigate the entire process of writing your world-changing book.

EXERCISE

Schedule eight 15-minute writing sessions in the next 30 days. Then keep those writing dates!

∽ *Part Three* ∽

DESIGN YOUR
WRITING PRACTICE

How do you actually make time and space over the long term to write a book? What must you shift to make this a priority? In part three, we look at designing a writing practice that will help you write your first book and others to come. What do I mean by a writing practice? A practice is a consistent activity that builds over time. A writing practice gives you:

- ❧ Self-confidence.
- ❧ The ability to hold the inner critic at bay more easily.
- ❧ A body of work.
- ❧ The ability to develop other life-enhancing practices like exercise and meditation.

Every time you honor your commitment to write, you make a deposit in your trust bank. You learn to trust and respect the part of you that wants to write.

Over time, you dedicate even more time to writing because you feel the benefits.

So much of the advice out there doesn't work because it's a one-size-fits-all approach. We try something on and when it doesn't fit, we (our inner critic) use it as evidence that we are a failure and should just give up.

Each person's writing practice will look different. In my work as a coach and writing mentor, I specialize in helping people design the practice that suits them and their goals. I like the adopt/adapt approach. Adopt suggestions and see how they fit. Then adapt them to your own needs and style. There's only one way to build a writing practice—to practice. When reading this section, consider how you will need to be both structured and flexible. Adopt my suggestions as an experiment. Tweak things. See what works for you. Soon you will develop your own writing practice that suits you and your lifestyle.

～ DESIGN A SUSTAINABLE ～ WRITING PRACTICE

During coaching sessions, my clients look at how to fit writing a book into their busy lives. We consider best days of the week, time of day and length of an average writing session. We spend a lot of time sorting this out. It all seems so reasonable and smart! The problem is, when clients are on the "coaching couch," they forget their other obligations. They forget about the holiday coming up, the visiting relatives or the extra workload they just took on.

What I have found after two decades of helping people write is that there is no perfect week for our writing. The routine we crave will be disrupted regularly. We want to set up structures and know what works best for us—and we have to be flexible.

Here's what I suggest to help you design a sustainable writing practice:

1. Imagine what your ideal or workable writing practice will look like. Assess what's feasible in your current circumstances.
2. Look at your calendar and determine your writing schedule for the next two weeks. Be sure to take

into account other obligations. Start small in your scheduling. Schedule 30 minutes and start the sessions with a 15-minute free-write. Set aside planning time too. (If you need to get your outline in order before you are able to settle down to the writing, see "Make Your Outline" in part four.) For these two weeks, stick to the plan.

3. Don't get waylaid by fear or perfectionism. Notice everything: how long you can sustain a focused writing session, what time of day works best for you, where you are most free to write. Record all of this in your notebook. Be curious and open. You are just getting to know your author self and her ways, so enjoy this getting-to-know-you process.

4. After two weeks, take a few moments to reflect on how things went. What worked? What did you notice? What will you tweak to have a writing practice that's truly yours? Don't berate yourself about any false steps or missed sessions. Just notice what choices you made, where you felt in the "zone" and where you felt flat. Then adjust accordingly.

5. Repeat this noticing process for another two weeks. By the end of 30 days of consistently showing up for your writing, you should have a clear sense of what works and what doesn't. You may have to adjust your writing schedule for travel or work plans, but you will have a solid base to start with. For longer-term planning, look at

the calendar and see what upcoming events are on there.

Travel, school obligations and other events can be seen as obstacles to scheduling writing time—or you can use them to support you and your book deadline. Let's say you are going on a trip May 1, and it's now March 4. Look at the calendar, taking into account all the things already on there. Count the number of writing sessions you can get in before May 1. You may think you have two months, but after subtracting weekends, workdays and other obligations, you might discover you really have only 10 writing sessions between now and your trip.

Big events can help you to focus on your project and set realistic goals over short periods of time. Monthly or quarterly goals help break things down into weekly goals.

While we like to think we will set up a detailed and structured creativity chastity belt to write our books, our practice will invariably ebb and flow with the rest of our commitments. A practice invites us to set aside judgment and focus on being present and doing our best. When we practice, we trust that when we consistently show up, the quality of the work will improve.

So be both a smart planner and an ardent opportunist. We will meet the ardent opportunist in the next chapter.

Exercise

What does your writing practice look like for the next 30 days? Write that down. Start each month and week identifying and calendaring your writing sessions. Start with an hour or less each time. Then keep the writing dates. Make dates that you can keep. Don't be overly optimistic here! What's important now is building self-trust. You want to build a sense of trust in yourself that you will stay connected to the book. Get in the habit of consulting your calendar and being real about how much writing time you actually have. This will help you to lower your expectations, get more done in the time you do have and feel regularly on top of the writing.

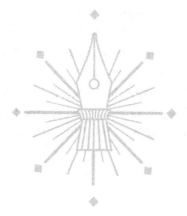

ᕲ Become an Ardent ᕲ
Opportunist

Relatives are in town. Something goes wonky in your mouth, requiring an emergency trip to the dentist. Your landlord decides it's time to give you notice. And then, to top it all off, the car breaks down and you spend your writing time at the repair shop. Because of these detours, nothing happens with your book, of course. Anyone would agree that you weren't able to focus. You are off the hook. Still, it's maddening that your life won't comply with your writing agenda! You hope that next week will be better once everything calms down. You can then resume your writing routine and finally get stuff done.

I get the frustration—I know how it is to have all the other things push themselves to the top of our agenda. But I hate to break it to you (actually, I love it): **there is no normal week**. The sh*t will hit the fan in one way or another on a weekly basis. On this you can count, my friend.

In the prior chapter, we talked about scheduling. That's all fine and good and will work. Some of the time. Some weeks will feel like a slog, others a sprint. **Become**

an ardent opportunist and watch your pages add up. Who is the ardent opportunist? She is both fierce and flexible. The ardent opportunist knows she can write anywhere, anytime, even if it's just capturing ideas and insights while away from the desk.

The ardent opportunist seizes any chance she can to write. She has her notebook with her at all times to capture her ideas, to whip out a 10-minute free-write, to finish a chapter. When an appointment cancels or a window of time opens up, she doesn't pop over to social media or email. She digs into her project, knowing that these small drips of time add up. The ardent opportunist savors little victories. Even the shortest sessions count, and she gives herself credit for showing up when she can.

The ardent opportunist doesn't make excuses. We can change our thoughts about the process to serve our goals. When random events throw her off course, she looks for ways to make them work for her. She sets deadlines and works hard to meet them. Sometimes, windows of time that we wouldn't have suspected to be fruitful can be very productive. Do you have these traits of an ardent opportunist? I am sure you will become one if you aren't already.

You are training yourself to put the book first. (Or at least second or third!) Make that your focus—getting to where the book is a priority. Some weeks will just suck. Often, right after you get into your writing groove, life will throw a wrench into the process. Don't despair! Do what you can and trust that you will make progress on your book, even if you feel like an inchworm.

EXERCISE

To get back on track with your book, set up a 15-minute quickie date. Give yourself no pressure to write and no need to make progress. Just reconnect with your book. Open the binder or document, read what you wrote last time and feel your way back into relationship with it. Make notes about what to work on next. Where will you resume? Make a note about your "insertion point." (Learn more about that soon in the chapter "Design Your Author Zones.")

— INQUIRY —

How have you been an ardent opportunist for your creative projects? For your book?

Get Back on Track

Because the sh*t will hit the fan, you will fall off your writing routine. I don't know anyone who has been able to stay on track like a Basset Hound on a scent of its prey, forever persistent and consistent. The problem is we spend so much time bemoaning that we have fallen off our focus and beating ourselves up about it. Don't fret! It's normal to fall off track. Learn to resume your writing with as minimal drag as possible. If you need to understand why you got derailed, reflect on these questions:

- When did you fall off your routine?
- What was going on in your life when you got off track?
- What were your thoughts and feelings about the book when you got derailed?
- What, in sum, can you notice about getting derailed?

Spend a brief time exploring the choices you have made. Be curious about what was underlying those choices. Then, get back at it. Keep showing up. In her book *One Continuous Mistake*, Gail Sher says that the only way to fail is to not show up. So if you have lost your groove and are feeling like a failure, shake it off and get back to it.

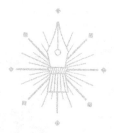

Set Yourself Up for Productive Writing Sessions

Your productivity and sense of your effectiveness will shift daily. There will always be days when you are frustrated and wish you could do more. Yet I believe that every bit of progress you make counts.

To cope with the feeling that you aren't doing enough on your book, start by identifying what "productive" means to you. Everyone is different in how they assess productivity. Determine how you will gauge your satisfaction about your productivity. Is word count most important? Or does tallying the number of hours you spend writing help you feel productive? Whatever meaningful metrics mean "productive" for you, identify them. **Set your own expectations so your inner critic isn't always hounding you to do more.**

My clients and students frequently say they need at least 30 minutes to get into the zone. This may be true, but it seems that the more cushion we give ourselves, the more time we waste. We check email, cruise Facebook and gradually fritter away our time focusing on stuff that's not truly necessary. The truth is, our time is a premium and we need to make the most of what we have.

There are many ways to integrate book writing into the flow of your days. If you don't really consider yourself a writer but the content of your book is also the focus of your work, you can make room for writing in your workday. A yoga teacher I coached found it easier to do a bit of writing directly after class, when her concepts were fresh in her mind. You might try this after meetings or lectures. Any time you have been sharing your work, it will be easier to capture those ideas on paper right away. If you work with clients or teach, keep a notebook open when working. If you say something that resonates strongly with a client, or find something you have offered to be particularly effective, make a note in your list of book ideas.

You can also start the day with a rendezvous with your book. You may need to set an alarm and get up early. If that scenario will never happen in your reality, perhaps you do your writing after everyone has gone to bed.

Here are a handful of strategies to help you design your most productive writing sessions. Adapt and adopt what suits you.

— BE SPECIFIC WHEN SCHEDULING —

Instead of having "write book" on your calendar, break it down. For instance, when I went to the café to work on this book one day, I knew I was only getting the chapter summaries down. My mission was to make it through the entire table of contents without delving too much into each chapter. I just wanted to get the gist of each chapter down in a few paragraphs.

— USE A CHECKLIST —

A checklist might work to help you easily transition and shed procrastination. Atul Gawande examines the power of a checklist in his book *The Checklist Manifesto*. When I learned how to scuba dive, a checklist was used to make sure all the gear was in working order. Perhaps you have a checklist that guides you into your writing zone. The items on your prep list could be:

- Turn off your notifications.
- Put your phone away, out of sight.
- Turn off internet access.
- Close all tabs on your browser.
- Set your timer.

Feel free to print up this list to keep in your writing zone. Or make your own checklist and use it to get in the groove easily. There are also many online programs to help you keep your focus. I have included them in the resources section.

— Warm up —

Use a series of free-writes to get going. Spend the first five minutes free-writing to clear your mind and set aside your other roles. Do another five minutes to warm up to your topic, to bring your focus to the book.

— Start small —

Give yourself 15–30 minutes to write your book. It's likely you will write for longer than 30 minutes, but if you give yourself 60, you will waste the first 30 minutes.

— Use an insertion point —

At the end of each writing session, make a note in your notebook or files pointing to where you will begin the next time. This is your insertion point. You can use a sticky note or a note in your digital system. In your document, write "INSERTION POINT" and simply search for that when you open your manuscript. Having an insertion point makes it easier to be an ardent opportunist.

— Take intentional breaks —

There's always a point where I lose the ability to focus. This usually happens 40–50 minutes into a writing session. I have learned to refuel myself with a 5–10 minute break and then dive back in for more writing. I stretch, go to the bathroom, play a round of online Scrabble. Then I write for another 30–40 minutes. These are your writing sprints. Pay attention to your focus scope—how long you typically hold your writing focus before needing a break. Honor your rhythms.

— MOVE AROUND WITHIN YOUR PROJECT —

Within the frame of your project, give yourself permission to bounce around. In this way, you can honor your need for variety but still stay focused. You might move among your chapters. Don't feel like you have to complete every word or section to be able to write other chapters.

See for yourself if moving among parts of your book works for you or if you need to maintain more focus on one chapter at a time. Perhaps you write in a more linear way. Your book may follow a chronological order, making a straightforward approach a better route. You will know very quickly whether your style is to go forward in a linear way or randomly through the book. Throughout drafts of the project, you will want to read from start to finish, to feel the flow of the book. But the book doesn't have to be written in that sequential way. See what works for you.

— EXPAND YOUR COMFORT ZONE —

Sometimes the writing process will confront you and you may feel uncomfortable. Your beliefs may be revealed, and this can be challenging.

You want to be able to easily and consistently drop into a focused state with your writing. When the work gets difficult, you may want to rebel against the focus, tempted to wander online, answer email, pop over to social media to get validation, and so on. Stay with it. Take a deep breath. Acclimate yourself and your system to longer and longer periods of focus.

— LIST IT —

Here's a practice that will help you manage all those other thoughts that intrude on your writing time. You will stay focused yet not feel constrained.

With your author notebook or pad of paper next to you when writing, capture ideas and thoughts that pounce the minute you try to focus. These could include a list of things to research for your writing. They could also include items for work or errands.

Keep two lists: ideas for the book and a list for everything else. When ideas come, jot them down on one of the lists and resume your writing immediately. Your mind won't stop its bouncy ways just because you have decided to focus, but you don't have to follow its jumbled path.

At the end of your writing session, check your lists that captured incoming thoughts. You may find that the things that seemed so urgent when they arose aren't that urgent. They were just distractions to your focus.

— INQUIRY —

What's your idea of a "productive session"? What helps you stay focused when writing?

⟲ DEFINE ⟳
YOUR AUTHOR ZONES

One of the challenges in writing a book is that we spend more time in the zones that aren't dedicated to writing. Our regular zones include home, office, car, kids' sports and extracurricular activities—and if you are like me, the grocery store. These places have been called "habit fields." The environments we occupy, with their own objects, orientations and sensations, habituate us to certain behaviors when we are there. So it makes sense that it's so hard to get any writing done at home when the laundry suddenly seems so compelling. We have perhaps not identified our author zone.

Where can we find a place to be in our author habit? We might have carved out a spot at home. Maybe our home office doubles as our writing zone. Or we have designed a writing cave in the basement, barricaded by the holiday decoration boxes and other stuff. Most of my clients have found that it's nearly impossible to inhabit the author role when they are in the habit field of their other roles.

I have been writing steadily for 25 years, and I have rarely been able to make significant progress in my home office. There are too many other activities in my other roles that vie for my attention. For me, writing in a café works best. I go to the café with a specific list of writing to do. I buy my cappuccino and set myself up. I pay my five-dollar coffee/focus fee and get going. In this space, I can't wander around. I feel like a jerk if I spend my café time prowling the internet or playing online Scrabble. It may seem pretentious to write in a café—I began doing it in my twenties as a way to be just like Hemingway. Over time, though, the café became my author zone, where I have written most of my books, articles and newsletters.

Your author zones may be seasonal. Your productivity may also respond to the seasons. Many of us feel more productive during the fall and winter months. When the weather forces us inside, it's easier to focus. During summer, I have a variety of author zones that allow me to get the work done and enjoy my favorite season. I write in the Orangerie at the Denver Botanic Gardens. I have been known to squeeze in a writing session at the local library. I even love being under a tree in the park.

Your place doesn't have to be the café. It could be the library, the stands of your kids' soccer games or in the car while your daughter is in dance class. The point of the author zone is that going there allows you to drop into your writing easily. You can write for a good 15 minutes or more with little or no distraction.

EXERCISE

Identify your author zone(s). Experiment with different options until you find the place where it's easiest to settle in to write.

Writing While Traveling

Are you a traveling writer? Some people can write easily while on the road. Others can't. Neither is better than the other; it's only important to know what works for you.

One client of mine loved his airplane time. It was the only place where he didn't have to respond to work demands. Where he wasn't responsible for his family's needs. Where he had uninterrupted time to write. He got a lot done while away from his routine. Others find that work trips, family trips or vacations are too disruptive to focus.

It doesn't matter if you can or can't write while away from home. What's damaging to your confidence is having unreasonable expectations for yourself. Bringing a lot of stuff with you to work on and not getting to it can add unnecessary stress. Remember, the main thing we need to guard and access is focus. Some people can focus more easily when away from home. Others find that they can't get much writing done while traveling. Decide which you are—a traveling writer or a home writer. Set your expectations accordingly.

$\backsim$ DEADLINES, $\sim$
GOALS AND MILESTONES

How do you feel about deadlines? Some of us love them and need that future date to get anything done. Others resist the structure, feeling pressured and resistant. Part of the problem may be how we think about our project along a timeline. I like to work with goals, milestones and deadlines to keep momentum. What's the difference between these things?

A goal is a specific outcome you can recognize when it has been achieved. "Complete the first draft of the book" is a goal. A milestone is a marker along the way to the goal. "Finished a chapter of the book draft" is a milestone. A deadline is a date-specific goal. "Complete a shaggy first draft by March 30" is a deadline.

Each of these is important to the book-writing process and can help you. A goal is a specific outcome. You will know when you have met your goal. The deadline helps you say no to additional projects while writing your book. The date can galvanize your focus, yet it may seem too far away to motivate you in the present moment. Milestones are the missing piece. When writing a book, these powerful markers along the way can help you feel and see a sense of progress.

In my coaching groups, we have weekly check-ins. On Mondays, we identify the specific work for the week. On Fridays, we celebrate the progress and the learning from our work. This weekly check-in process helps break projects into small, actionable steps. Every week we get to feel a sense of progress. This consistent honoring of milestones builds our confidence and satisfaction long before the goal is met.

Deadlines give me something to work toward. If I don't meet the deadline, I am not deterred. What matters is that I am making engaged, consistent progress toward the goal.

You can plan your days and weeks around your deadline. Keep your goal in mind and use milestones to send up flares of joy, celebrating even small victories. This may seem inconsequential, but when you are working on a project that will possibly take years, those milestones matter.

Deadlines can be a great ally in creating boundaries with your peeps. People understand the importance of the word "deadline." When you get a request to do something that isn't contributing to finishing your book, you can use the magic phrase that works almost every time: "I'm on deadline." It's short, it's sweet, it requires no explanation and people get it. Try it out and see how well it works to hold your boundaries and your writing focus.

— INQUIRY —

How can you use milestones, deadlines and goals to finish your book?

VITAL PRACTICES TO
SUPPORT YOUR WRITING

All of our choices contribute to our ability to do our work. Each part of our life contributes to the whole. During book-coaching sessions with my clients, we address these various life issues together.

Your lifestyle choices are up to you, and I don't presume to know the right way for you to live. But I do know that consistent practices or habits can contribute to making it easier to focus, follow through and finish your book. Here are a few practices that my clients find have contributed to their productivity.

— STILLNESS PRACTICE —

People always told me I should meditate. But the thought of sitting obediently never appealed to me. Oddly, it was when a friend described meditation as a *stillness practice* that it actually appealed to me. For some reason, phrasing it this way seemed more of an invitation. So I started, slowly, with five minutes and then 10 minutes. Over time, I built up my ability to sit and just be.

Now when I meditate, my mind still races and I am fidgety. I'm no perfect meditator. But I do appreciate the opportunity to becalm myself at the beginning of the day. Starting quietly and slowly makes my days seem more spacious. I don't jump into action and urgency.

Practicing stillness at the beginning of the day also is a time to be receptive to inner wisdom and guidance. You might ask a question or set an intention for your book. If you are struggling with something, you could ask for guidance and sit with it, patiently awaiting the answer. Maybe you use an oracle deck, tarot or angel cards to access insights.

You may not sit still. Your practice might look like an early morning walk. Or an extra 10 minutes in bed. Whether sitting for a few minutes or moving, make space for your wisdom and insights to land.

— PHYSICAL PRACTICE —

I believe that a consistent physical practice can give us more space to receive our best ideas and associations. Yoga, walking, aqua aerobics, jogging—**whatever moves you will also move your writing**.

I love blending a physical practice into my book writing. I do some writing, then take a walk or do other exercise. Ideas and insights marinate and develop when I am moving. Afterward, I make notes in my notebook.

You know that exercise helps you feel great, look great and sleep well. Guess what? It helps you be a better writer too.

— SPIRITUAL PRACTICE —

You may or may not be religious or spiritual, but I have found that the clients who have some kind of connection to the Divine or a universal perspective fare better when the going gets tough. A spiritual practice helps us stay connected to our soul work, operating from a deeper place than our ego or personality. With a spiritual connection, we can more easily tap into a bigger purpose than our own personal or professional gains. When we waver or doubt our abilities, touching in with our spiritual self can restore our confidence and commitment. World-changing books often come from a bigger devotion or commitment than just our own agenda. And a spiritual connection is sometimes part of that bigger purpose. If you don't feel moved in a particular spiritual or religious way, no problem. You can still write your book.

EXERCISE

Write down the practices that contribute to your book writing. Be specific about why they are vital to your creative work.

Don't Let Research Hijack Your Focus

You are jamming away at your book, composing merrily, when you realize you need more information—a date, a name, the specific thing that will shore up an argument in your book. You jump online, searching away. Before you know it, you have spent 40 minutes leaping from link to link, gathering more research.

Finding information for your book online, what I call *re-surfing*, is fun. You can claim, guilt free, that you are working on your book. But a glance at the clock shows it's time to pick up the kids. You end your session and enter the slipstream of your busy day. Your one-hour writing session involved exactly 20 minutes of writing and 40 minutes of re-surfing, yielding a couple of scribbled pages and a lot of information, much of it not applicable to your book. Sound familiar?

I know this scenario well. Having written a historical novel, I have spent countless hours researching my era and time period. The time we spend researching may seem legit, but it could be a cleverly disguised inner critic. **It's much easier to surf an endless research loop than to do the difficult work of writing.** It's safer to read others' stuff than to generate our own material.

Your inner critic loves that you are spending so much time looking at other people's work. It's committed to making sure you don't look like a fool. However, your dedication to excellence and thoroughness can all too easily tip into the inner critic territory of self-doubt and never-achievable perfection that can prohibit you from ever getting your book done.

It doesn't have to be this way. Try the following simple but effective practices to keep your research efforts from becoming the purview of the critic.

EXERCISE

Set aside a specific amount of time each week for research. Be realistic—one or two hours is usually enough. If you have only two hours a week to work on your book, give one and a half hours to writing and half an hour to research.

While writing, keep a separate log of items that need to be researched. When an issue comes up (what kind of fabric were skirts made of in 1937?), jot that down on your research list. Keep a page in your notebook or a digital document titled "To research."

Know when you have the most focus for writing and when research is a better use of your time. I usually do research at the end of the week in the afternoon, when my focus for writing wanes.

If you are writing a nonfiction book based on your expertise, consider drafting your material *before* looking to see what others have written. Get a sense of how much you need to know about what's out there before you feel confident claiming your authority. People fall into the trap of spending a lot of time researching the field and then never write their own book.

If necessary, make time to seek copyright clearance. For writers using others' images, lyrics, poems and other protected works, getting permission to use this material takes time and money. Getting permissions can take months. Get started on that early. For my novel, I wanted to use a poem by Stephen Spender, a real person and a character in my book. I sought out the Stephen Spender Trust, sent my request, and paid a small fee for using the poem in my book.

Keep a list of sources—websites, magazines, people—that you will turn to for information. Be open to the fun serendipity that will lead you beyond what you know and into territory that will enhance your book. Notice when the impulse to research arises. It frequently surfaces just as you sit down to write. But notice too, how your focus and energy and perhaps even your confidence can diminish the more time you spend in research mode. While research may be vital for our books, it's never more important than the writing itself. Keep the two in balance.

— INQUIRY —

What's your plan for keeping your research process in balance with your writing?

Build Deliberate
Competence

Writing a book is a whole different animal than writing a blog or an article. Obviously, it's longer. A book allows you to delve more deeply into your material. It will contain the bulk of your ideas on your topic. There may be many facets of your topic, many channels of thoughts and ideas. You can include them all. One of the gifts of writing a book is that you aren't restricted to making it short as you are with a blog post.

Many of my clients come to book writing with a lack of confidence in their ability to pull off the whole enchilada. One of the things they are concerned about is whether the book will be long enough. I say it doesn't matter how long it is; it just has to be to the point and of service. Sometimes a shorter book is best for the subject matter and readers' needs.

Your sense of competency will wax and wane as you write the book. This is normal. One day you will feel like you absolutely have this down. The next day you will be certain the world will think you are a fraud. Don't get distracted or invested in these emotional thoughts. Don't try to prove them wrong or wallow in the notion that you are indeed an imposter. Your writing days will likely be accompanied by these thoughts; the quicker you can sit down and write, the better. Perhaps you have already written something. Maybe you have blogged or written articles for your business or work. Look at your writing history to date and draw confidence from that. What do you know about yourself as a writer? What do you appreciate about your style? Look at your subject matter competence. You have earned some credibility from that. Borrow from your previous writing wins and competency to fuel your book-writing confidence. Soon you will have confidence from writing your book. Keep your writing dates and steadily build your competence and confidence.

--- INQUIRY ---

What have you done that you can draw upon to build your book-writing confidence?

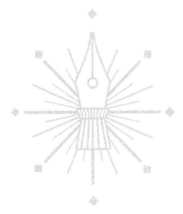

∽ *Part Four* ∾

Manage Your Content

Managing the material for your book—organizing the contents and deciding what goes where—can be quite daunting. Writing a book is a messy process. Oddly, the book has a life of its own. I know that sounds woo-woo, but I have seen it happen over and over. You set out to write the book, moving material around, with an idea of how it will look and what it will contain. And then the book shape-shifts and becomes something different. You realize you aren't the person in charge, but a collaborator with the material. The sooner you surrender to this notion, the better. Still, we need to take the reins and rally our thoughts, our material and our words. Let's dive in.

IDENTIFY YOUR READER

If you have a business, you have no doubt spent time identifying your ideal client or customer. This is known as your "avatar." When you know what motivates them and understand the problem your product or service solves, it's easier to design things that you know they will need, buy, love and rave about. Perhaps your avatar is simply another version of you. Many people have built wildly successful businesses making things that they themselves need and want. If your ideal customer is another version of you, you are in luck. You know your needs and desires—and your challenges—very well. Even if you don't have a business, you still want to know who you are writing for.

When writing a nonfiction book, you must have clarity about your ideal reader. What title would make them pick it up? What words on the back of the book make it a must-buy right now? And what would make them tell their friends about it too? It's important to know these things, not just from a marketing perspective but from a writing perspective. Often when we sit down to write, we become overly formal and lose touch with our voice and our confidence.

When we have a clear sense of who the ideal reader is, it's easier to write directly to them. Write in a conversational tone as if you are having coffee together and you are telling them everything you want them to know about your topic. Ideally, this is a real person you know. Having a real, specific person in mind will make all the difference. Your writing will flow, and decisions will feel easy to make. And yet, you will resist it. You will want the book to be for everybody. You will think of three or more separate audiences for whom your book would be of interest.

That's the problem—it's not for an "audience." When you think of that word, what comes to mind is probably a bunch of people or a big group. But when you think of one specific person and the problem this book is solving, you will make writing your book infinitely easier. Trust me. I understand that you can see your book's value for different kinds of people. You want to be inclusive, but for your book's focus I want you to be exclusive. Your book is not for everyone. You aren't pleasing everyone.

Let's use a target model to drive this concept home. Suppose you are writing a book about how women can fit exercise into their life. Now identify up to three kinds of readers for your book. You want it for busy moms because you are a busy mom and you know that your methods work for you and your friends. You also want more people to have this information. Heck, *everybody* needs this! But for now, choose just three potential readers. These three types of readers could be busy moms, college students and business owners.

If you try to write to all three kinds of readers, your writing will go all over the place. Imagine a target. Put your main reader in the center ring. Your next type of reader goes in the second ring, and so on. When you write to hit the heart of the target, you meet your main reader and their needs. Anyone else picking up the book could also find value. With your main reader in mind, you won't be without direction.

I cannot emphasize how important it is to have this very specific person in mind when you are writing.

Exercise

Take some time to free-write about your ideal reader, the one who needs your book and will recognize it when they see it. Give them a name and get very clear about who they are and why your book is important to them. Write a letter to your reader about how your book will help them live a better life. Tell them that you are excited to share this information and why you are the perfect person to do so. Now print that up and keep it in your writing zone so you are always writing to them. Include a picture of them if you can. Later, some of what you have written could be useful in your marketing copy. Next, we will look at the issues your book solves for your reader.

— Inquiry —

What resistance, if any, comes up for you when I ask you to choose a specific reader?

∽ DELVE INTO THE ∽
PROBLEMS YOUR BOOK SOLVES

Now that you have identified your reader, you want to be sure that your book is solving one or more of their problems. Yes, you, being useful and helping your reader live a better life! That's why you are writing this book, right? Don't play small! Claim the fact that your book will change lives. Most nonfiction books are meant to solve a specific problem.

Scan the titles on your bookshelves and identify what problems they address. **The title or subtitle of your book should clearly deliver a promise of the difference your book will make for your reader.** When I chose the title of this book, I knew it was for women who have multiple roles to play and who have specific needs for those roles.

The Busy Woman's Guide to Writing a World-Changing Book solves two problems:

◇ My reader—that's you!—has wanted to write a book for a long time. It's one of those bucket-list items that simply won't go away. **One problem my book solves is helping my**

reader know how to structure her time, focus her attention and wrangle her material into a book.

◇ It takes time to write a book, and my reader is busy. She doesn't necessarily have long afternoons at coffee shops to write. She might not be able to get away for a writing retreat. She may only have a few minutes here or there or a short window of time on the weekends to write her book. **The second problem my book solves is gearing solutions toward my reader's specific needs.** I know she doesn't have a lot of extra time in the day, so I offer suggestions for writing the book in short spurts. I give specific ways to drop into the writing easily so as not to waste precious writing time.

We love helping others, and your book is here to change worlds. Start with your reader's world and change it one chapter at a time. You may change just one thing for her. Maybe it's a small thing that has a big impact. Know that your book will have a positive impact, even if will help just one person. That counts.

Exercise

Let's go back to your reader. What problems keep them up at night? What issues continue to plague them? Make a list, or mind-map all the challenges your reader has around your specific topic. Then make another list of their challenges that may not relate to your topic. Perhaps they have a hard time finding help around the house. Maybe their financial picture isn't so pretty. What are the issues you know they grapple with? If you work with individual clients or groups, consult your notes from your time with these people. You may find recurring themes and issues there. You will also see the solutions you offered. This information can provide great material for your book.

After you have made the lists, look at your table of contents. Be sure you are solving at least five of your reader's problems related to your topic. Your book may also address your reader's other challenges. It will be easier to write when you think of each piece being useful to them.

— Inquiry —

What problems does your book address?

Choose the Software for Your Writing

Organizing your material is one of the biggest challenges you will face in writing your book. You will need to make a decision about how to manage the content and files. There are a number of software programs that make this easier. I will share what I have used and what my clients have found useful.

Warning! Sometimes people learn a new software program as a way to procrastinate writing. It can take forever to set themselves up. Don't get caught in this seemingly productive procrastination trap!

If this chapter doesn't make sense yet or isn't relevant to how you are writing a book, that's okay. It's intended as a brief overview, not a comprehensive comparison.

— Evernote —

I write everything in Evernote. This cloud-based software is very simple to use. It uses "notebooks" to organize files into categories. When I write a book, I create a notebook with the book's title. I use a series of "notes" that go into that notebook to write each chapter.

I have the book's outline in a note, and after I write a chapter, I make that chapter title bold in the outline. (That way I know it's done.) This outline serves as a to-do list as much as a table of contents. When it's time to write a new chapter, I copy the title into a new note, and that note becomes the draft for that chapter. The notebook contains the chapters of the book, each chapter in its own note.

There may be additional notebooks for the book. A series of notebooks on a topic in Evernote is called a "notebook stack." There may be a "research notebook" with a series of notes containing items I have clipped and saved related to the book. There's a "Cut from book" note where I keep snippets I have excised. I rarely use them, but it helps knowing they aren't thrown away completely.

I compose in Evernote because I like how simple it is to see my chapter notes. They are separate from each other, and it's easy to revise and rewrite in these documents. If I had all the chapters in one big document, the scrolling and searching would be Dante's 10th ring of hell. It's just too much to manage while I am in the early drafts. Finally, Evernote backs up my work automatically, saving me from having to remember that step.

— GOOGLE DOCS —

Google Docs is a free, web-based app. A big benefit of choosing Google Docs is that users can collaborate with others on documents.

When I have a complete, albeit shaggy, draft of each of the notes in Evernote, I go online and create a document in Google Docs. I copy and paste each note into one document, following the order of the outline, which has now become the table of contents (TOC). I am careful to keep the name of each chapter exactly as it appears in the TOC, until I have edited and fine-tuned those titles. I then make a separate document for the TOC because it's easier to pop back and forth between documents than to scroll through the entire doc to get back to the TOC.

At this point, I can number the pages and print the whole document in one go. (Printing from Evernote is a pain because the note titles don't always appear on the pages and you cannot add page numbers in Evernote.)

Google Docs allows me to easily share the draft and ask for feedback. Readers can make comments and editing suggestions that are easy to see and respond to. Embedding images in Google Docs is also fairly straightforward.

You can use Google Docs to compose your entire book, using the same method I described for Evernote. Both are cloud-based, so if you are away from your computer and want to make a note or do a quick writing session on your phone or tablet, you can do it right in your existing structure. No need for random notes written on envelopes; your book is always with you.

Google Docs also has a really cool Voice Typing feature that allows you to speak your book and have it dictated onto the page. I use this when I am writing something but don't feel like actually typing or don't feel the words right there at the tip of my fingers. In a Google Doc, go to Tools>Voice Typing. Hit the microphone on the left and speak. Watch your words appear on the screen and voilà. You may write your entire book this way. Of course, some editing will be required.

As with Evernote, Google Docs automatically backs up your work. You should, however, manually back up your work to an external drive on a regular basis. You never know when/if something will happen. It's always better to be safe than sorry; back up your work weekly.

— SCRIVENER —

A lot of my clients use Scrivener to write their books. The "index card" system helps them organize their material in a visual way.

In Scrivener, each section of your manuscript is connected to a virtual index card. You can rearrange your manuscript by moving individual cards around in your table of contents. It may take considerable time to familiarize yourself with Scrivener's many tools and settings. If you are a quick learner and don't get distracted by a steep learning curve, go for Scrivener.

I personally don't use Scrivener to write my books. I prefer the simpler Evernote and Google Docs. Maybe I am too impatient, but I want the quickest path to me and the writing. I don't want to spend a lot of time figuring out the new software.

The great thing about being a writer today is that Aunty Google has answers for helping you choose which program to use to write your book. Many people have written about the programs I have discussed, and you can do a search to compare what they say and see what system is right for you. Ask writing buddies what works for them. If you are already using one of them (or another program) and like it, continue with that. No need to add something new to the mix.

Exercise

Choose one software system and stick with it. Don't let the choosing/on-boarding process delay your writing.

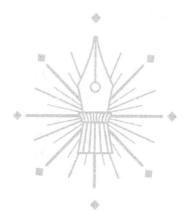

◌ DETERMINE ◌
THE STRUCTURE OF YOUR BOOK

By now you have probably wondered about your book's structure. Having a sense of the structure will help you know how to approach writing the book. That makes sense, but the book's final structure might not be what you start with. In fact, most of the books I have written or helped others write end up looking nothing like their original vision. That's okay. Still, you must start somewhere.

What's the best structure for your book? Here are some possibilities:

- Personal narrative or memoir.
- Narrative nonfiction.
- How-to or self-help book based on your expertise.
- Inspirational daybook.
- Book of your art or photography.
- Fiction: either a collection of short stories or a novel.

You already know the problems the book is solving. **Knowing your reader, how do you think they**

will interact with the material? Will they read in short bursts? Will they take a bigger chunk of time on a weekend? Or read on long airplane flights? Will they take notes? Are they reading a paper book or a digital book? Perhaps they aren't reading at all, but listening to audio books instead. When you know the answers to these questions, you will see how your reader will be experiencing your material. You will know whether you will be working mainly with text or also with images, videos and/or hyperlinks.

Depending on your goals, your material could exist in several forms, offering readers different ways to interact with it. There are many ways your work could reach your readers, starting with a print edition and/or e-book and later bringing the basic material into online classes, webinars, podcast episodes, lectures, retreats, and much more.

As you dig deeper into the content, your project will dictate its own path. With almost every client I have coached, **the project morphs when the author allows the material to influence the form.** Don't endlessly try to construct the ideal form in your mind. Plunge in and let the content lead the way.

It can help to look at comparable titles. Check out your bookshelf. Pull out a few books you love. Might one of them have a similar structure that would suit your book? Make notes about what you love about the book, taking into account its size, shape, fonts, layout, chapter content, chapter length and images (if any).

When I wrote my first book, *Create Your Writer's Life,*

I used Julia Cameron's *The Artist's Way* as a structural guide. I liked the elements she included and used some of them in my book.

No matter what the final form, I suggest free-writing as the way to get your first thoughts out on the page. Remember, you can use free-writing to draft material and also to sort out questions and puzzles you are solving about the book's format. With these preliminary ideas to work with, you can see what you need to add or take away to hone your message.

EXERCISE

Look at books you like, noting the elements that the author included. What might you adopt/adapt? Based on your reader and how this person reads, determine a structure to start with.

MIND-MAP YOUR TOPIC

Managing the contents of our book can be a real challenge. There's so much to say, and we wonder if we are adding too much, going off on a tangent or making any sense at all.

Many people recommend making an outline, which I talk about in the next chapter. Using an outline for nonfiction books helps writers fill in the table of contents with their ideas. But most of my clients don't start with an outline. Why not? Because an outline is an orderly, linear thing, and most of us don't think in orderly, linear ways.

I suggest starting the content gathering with a mind-mapping process. Mind-mapping helps to get all the material out of your head and onto the page. You can see the materials you have to work with. When you see them, you can start to organize them. With your book topics, you will start to see which ideas belong together and how the whole might take shape. For now, we are just getting the ideas out where we can see them.

There are several ways to do this. Try one of the following methods and see what works for you.

- **Use paper or a whiteboard to mind-map ideas.** In the center of the page or whiteboard,

write the basic premise of your book in large
letters. This could be your working title.
Then add bubbles or lines, one topic or idea
per bubble/line. Your ideas will start to form
clusters as you add similar ideas in bubbles/lines
adjacent to each other. There may be several
large categories. For each category, capture the
ideas you have for that category.

- **Mind-map using index cards or sticky
  notes.** The mind-mapping process is the
  same here, but using index cards/sticky notes
  allows you to move your ideas around if you
  find they belong with a different category than
  you originally thought. You may want several
  colors of index cards or sticky notes to color-
  code different types of content categories that
  are in your book: red for explication, green for
  example stories, yellow for exercises. Write your
  ideas on the index cards or sticky notes, each
  idea on its own card or note. Use a corkboard or
  wall to tack up your ideas.

- **Create a digital mind map.** You can also
  use software like MindMeister to make digital
  mind maps. These mind maps can be easily
  accessed and adjusted.

Mind-mapping your topic, using whichever method you
prefer, will help you begin to clarify the contents of your
book.

EXERCISE

Brainstorm your ideas using the mind-mapping method. See how it works for you. Keep playing until you are out of ideas. Go take a break and come back to see it afresh. What do you notice about your content? Which categories have the most ideas? Which ideas or categories feel most compelling to you? Make a star or put a sticker on those so they stand out. Let this settle for a few days, adding to it and moving things around until you feel you have most of your ideas on paper and where you want them to be for now.

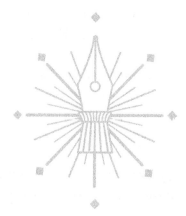

ᡣᢠ Make Your Outline ᢠᡣ

Once you have created your mind map (see the prior chapter for instructions), you are ready to make your outline.

Take your major categories from your mind map and divide them into sections, with all the smaller ideas or stories under each section. Ask yourself: What *must* be in the book? What must my readers know? It's fine if you don't have a 100 percent complete outline at this point. Don't overwork it.

Be warned! People can have so much fun with the planning and outlining process that they never move to the writing phase. Then, when they do go to write, they find that their engagement with the material is very low. They have expended all their energy in the planning process.

Even if you don't know all the pieces that will go into your book, that's okay. Through writing it, you will get a sense of what's missing and what must be included.

Don't spend more than 10 days mind-mapping and outlining. I mean it! Get a working outline in place and then start writing. Don't use up all your creative energy in planning.

EXERCISE

Make an outline, even if it's rough and incomplete.
It will help you get started with the writing.

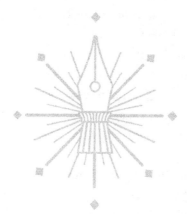

ORGANIZE YOUR MATERIAL
WITH A CHAPTER TEMPLATE

Earlier in part four, you got a sense of the structure your book might take, and you may feel more at ease. Yet you still need to organize your material. It can help to develop a chapter template. A chapter template contains the elements that will appear in each chapter. For instance, a chapter template could include the following:

- **An introduction.** This is an overview of the chapter, and it clarifies why the reader needs the information that will be covered.
- **The main content.** This constitutes the body of the chapter.
- **Inspirational quotations.** Some books include inspiring quotations.
- **Stories.** Many books include stories to illustrate the point the author is making. Case studies, examples from your own experience, and research can help readers access the information in different ways.
- **Suggested activities for the reader.** These could appear throughout the text or in a list at the end of the book.

- **A chapter summary.** It has become a common practice to provide an end-of-chapter summary with the key takeaways of that chapter. This is helpful in books that have a lot of research and data.
- **Illustrations or images.** Will your book include visual elements? Photos? Illustrations? Line drawings? Not every book is served by images. Does your book need visual elements?

Using insights you gleaned from looking at your favorite books, list the elements you want to see in each of your chapters and your reason why. You don't need a lot of different elements, just the ones that will be useful to your reader. Once you nail down your chapter template, draft a complete sample chapter to see how each element builds upon and increases the impact of your work.

With a chapter template, it will be so much easier to write/fill in the other chapters. No more guessing what goes in each one!

EXERCISE

Take your time developing a template that includes the elements you want in each chapter. Don't worry if this takes some time. You are choosing the bones of your book and you want to make sure you are including everything.

Next, draft a sample chapter to see how it flows. Adjust the content as needed. Once you have this sample chapter written, you will be able to more easily write the remaining chapters.

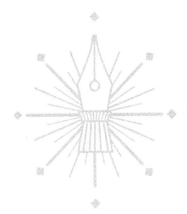

DRAFT CHAPTER SUMMARIES

Returning to your book outline now, you can loosely flesh it out by writing short chapter summaries. Writing chapter summaries gives you a sense of the content in each chapter and helps to minimize repetition. You can write the summaries in one document or in separate documents, one for each chapter.

I wrote chapter summaries for this book—each chapter had its own document. I quickly jotted down the point of each one. Then, when I went to write, I knew what was going to go into each chapter. The summaries were guidelines to keep me focused. For your chapter summaries, ask yourself:

- What purpose is this chapter serving in the book?
- What *must* go in this chapter?

EXERCISE

Write brief, four-sentence summaries for every chapter. You can do this in the outline if you wish, but it can become unwieldy. I like to keep the outline clean and easy to scroll through.

Get Help Shaping Your Material

Many writers hire someone to help them sort out the content and organization of a book. It's not easy to wrangle all of our ideas into book form. Work with a developmental editor early on—after you draft your outline or produce a shaggy first draft—in other words, before you have gotten too far along. This kind of support comes before you give anything to beta readers.

An outside, professional perspective can help you write a book that meets your goals and communicates your message. A developmental editor looks at the overall book to determine whether each chapter contributes to the whole and that the organization works. This person could be a book coach. I hired a book coach to help me develop a book proposal. We had a couple of meetings, and she reviewed my proposal drafts and helped me to shape and communicate my ideas more clearly. The time and money spent to hire her was invaluable.

If you are stuck with organizing your thoughts, consider working with someone to help you wrangle your material.

IDENTIFY YOUR BOOK'S PROMISE WITH COVER COPY

You might find it easier to keep your materials focused if you have written the jacket copy for the back cover. This is a piece of sales or marketing writing, letting the reader know what to expect when they read your book. When I write jacket copy, I like to think of it as the "promise," the through line of what I am offering my readers.

Not only does writing jacket copy serve as a compass for keeping you on track, it helps to establish your authority and solidify in the reader's mind and in your mind why you are the person to write the book. Even the most established experts can lose their confidence while writing a book. This piece of writing will help you maintain your cool and remind you of your purpose for writing your book.

Look at a couple of your favorite books as examples. Your book's jacket copy should include these things:

- What problems your book solves.
- How your book's approach is different than other solutions.
- Why you are the person to write this book.

- ꙮ An overview of what's in the book.
- ꙮ Blurbs from clients or people in your field highlighting your expertise.
- ꙮ A one-paragraph author bio that speaks to your authority in the book's subject.

Keep this list handy when writing your copy. It will remind you what to include and what to leave out. It will also keep you aligned with your book's true north. This list will serve many, but not all, types of books. For instance, if you are writing a memoir, you might not have a clear sense of the whole until you have finished it. Insights you glean along the way will inform your copy.

Whatever the genre, if you can write the copy for the back of the book, it can serve as a guide to keep you focused on what you are communicating with your reader. Don't worry if marketing writing is not your specialty. You can work with someone later to help with that part. For now, get something on paper. This is your promise of what you are offering your readers.

Exercise

Write the jacket copy for your book. Keep your target reader and their problems in mind. This may take several versions. Don't rush it and don't be frustrated if it takes more time than you think to get this down.

DRAFT A WORKING TITLE

When we set out to write our book, we may not have a title for it yet. We know what our book is about, sure, but we haven't committed to a title.

Choosing a working title will make writing your book easier. The title will likely change over time, but having one early on will help you draft your book. With a working title, you can call it by its name. Saying you are writing *Claim Your Authority* is much more powerful than saying you are writing a book. **The working title is another compass to help orient you.** If you are considering adding material to the book, you can always look at the working title and ask yourself if the new material fits under that title.

Having a working title is also a way to *own* the book. It becomes one step closer to real. When you go to work on your book, you can put the title in your calendar. This makes it more specific and real. Sharing your title with people like your ideal reader can serve as market research.

When I mentioned the title of this book to likely readers, they immediately said, "I want that book now!" That added to my motivation to write it. A word of caution, though: be careful not to talk about your book too, too much. Sometimes when we talk about our book all over the place, we get unwelcome feedback or spend our writing energy blabbing about it. As for the title, don't fret over it. Just find one that works for you now.

EXERCISE

Come up with a working title that feels good to you, that conveys the gist of your book. Your working title might even make you smile or give you a boost when you think about it. Use it in your document, your calendar and your conversations.

⌒ WRITE A MANIFESTO ⌒
FOR YOUR BOOK

When I talked with colleagues about my idea for this book, I felt the fire and the passion of what I wanted to share with my readers. I knew what I wanted to say. This excitement was followed by the impulse to write an introduction, a "what this is about"—something that rang true, that would incite joy and possibility and empowerment. The logical approach would be to start with the beginning, or so I thought. But when I sat down to write my introduction, the idea of drafting something that big and meaningful completely shut me down. My writing felt stiff and formal.

This happens to my clients all the time. Writing the introduction can seem like a huge task—too much to gather in one chapter. An introduction is an explanation of what's to come. However, you may not know what exactly will be in your book, so it can be better to write the introduction *after* you have written the book. Here's my solution: write a manifesto for your book instead of the introduction.

A manifesto is about the impact that you want your book to have on your readers. Thinking about what you want for them will help you get away from the work being about you. This can help you overcome fears and insecurities. **A manifesto is a stake—what you are taking a stand for.** It can be used for your work outside the book if you do workshops or book tours, for example.

Even though the difference between a manifesto and an introduction is clear, it can still feel difficult to sit down and draft your manifesto. The following exercise, which I use with my clients, helped me identify what I wanted to say in this book.

Imagine that you are speaking to your main reader. They are smiling at you, sending love and appreciation. They are eager to hear what you have to say. You have five minutes to tell them what you want to share. Answer these three questions to get to the heart of your work:

◇ What do you want for your reader?
◇ What must they know now?
◇ What do you want them to do with the knowledge you have given them?

See yourself speaking to your people from your heart, as if this were your one and only opportunity to do so. The time is now. The need to share your work is urgent.

Feel free to speak your manifesto aloud and record it. You can play it back later. There are a number of dictation tools out there. Try Dragon Dictation software, Voice Typing in Google Docs, or another recording program. Or just speak, then type like mad what you have written.

I believe that for this kind of writing, if you aren't crying or nearly crying, you haven't dug deep enough to write what's truly meaningful for you. Imagining a direct and sincere communication with the people you are writing for can lead you past insecurities that are common at this stage.

EXERCISE

Write a manifesto for your book. Drafting your manifesto can help you focus on your work as a gift to your people instead of serving as a reflection on how great you are. Your manifesto will help you get out of your own way and hush your inner critic. It may take several drafts, and it may take time. Don't worry about it. Just get the essence of it out and keep going.

Manifesto for *The Busy Woman's Guide to Writing a World-Changing Book*

Books can change lives. Books are powerful.
Women are powerful. When women write books, their power grows and inspires others.
Women and books make a power pair.
Now is the time to bring your wisdom, your truth, your expertise and your power to light. Women's voices are ringing more loudly and truly than ever.
Bring your power into your world-changing book. Write it now.
Change the world with your book.

∽ Part Five ∽

WRITE AND FINISH
YOUR BOOK

As I have said, it will take time to sort out what goes into your book and how to organize it. BUT! Let me remind you: don't spend all of your time organizing the outline. This is a pitfall many of my clients fall prey to. It's easier to be in the higher-level thinking of organizing and sorting. Settling in to do the work of writing is another story. So please, don't stay in planning mode for more than a couple of weeks.

Books sort themselves out through the writing, not through endless organizing. Even in the final drafts of this book, I was reorganizing based on how the writing flowed (or didn't). The final result wasn't perfectly mapped to my outline, and your book won't look like you first imagined or planned it either.

Ready to write? This is where it gets fun!

Write from
Your Prompts

In part two's "Gather Your Project-Based Writing Prompts," you learned ways to capture your ideas in one place related to your book project. Now that you have your content and ideas mapped out, you can use those items as prompts for your free-writing sessions. Your prompts may be the items in your outline. If so, you can free-write from those prompts, going from beginning to end. Or you can free-write from prompts you jotted on index cards. Some people like to progress linearly; others prefer a random process. Order will come through the writing.

For this book, I used my table of contents to write drafts of each chapter, one by one. When I completed a free-write draft of a chapter, I made that chapter topic bold in the outline. I could easily scan and see which topics were done and which ones were unwritten.

If you are using index cards to hold your prompts (as mentioned in part four, "Mind-Map Your Topic"), when you have written that topic, remove them from your cork-board or turn them over so the blank side is showing. I prefer to remove them so I can visually see myself making progress. This visual tracking is important. Writing a book is a long haul, and being able to see visual progress can help our morale. It also helps us to know where we are in the process.

— INQUIRY —

What do you notice when you write from your prompts?

❧ FREE-WRITE ❧
YOUR SHAGGY FIRST DRAFT

Although there are many ways to get our writing out, I swear by one simple but potent approach to writing anything: free-writing. As I mentioned earlier, I have taught this method to hundreds of people because it's so simple yet so powerful. Not only does it banish writer's block for good, it also helps change our lives for the better. You will love how liberating this process is.

Free-writing will help you get a shaggy first draft out so you have something you can refine. If you try to write well in the first draft, you are writing and editing at the same time. These two processes are necessary, but doing them simultaneously is painstaking, squelches your true voice and makes your inner critic the queen of your project. And we know how painful that can be. I like thinking of it as a shaggy draft, held together with maybe some gaps and dangling strings. But it will be enough to work with for the second draft. This first draft isn't supposed to be 100 percent sparkling and complete. Go for shaggy and finished over perfect and incomplete.

—— What's free-writing? ——

I talked about free-writing in the "Get Started Writing" guide (see "Make Free-Writing Your Power Tool" in part two). I have been free-writing everything since 1994, when I learned this method in a writing class in Denver. I have been teaching it since 1996, both in person and in my online classes.

I am not the kind of person who insists that my way is *the* way. But I have seen hundreds of people use this method to finally quiet their inner critic long enough to get their words onto the page.

Writer's block stinks. You feel an urge to write. Maybe you even have your material outlined. But everything else gets in the way and your writing sits inside you, trapped. This unexpressed writing can feel incredibly painful. We all go through this, but we don't have to stay stuck. Free-writing can help alleviate some suffering. Free-writing does all these things:

- Hushes the inner critic that says you don't know how to write or don't have anything to say.
- Makes it easy peasy to get started.
- Releases insecurities about spelling, punctuation or grammar.
- Helps you overcome the difficulty of sitting down and focusing.
- Allows you to make the most of short bursts of time.
- Gives you the satisfaction of seeing your words add up on the page.

I could go on and on! I love, love, love teaching this method. My students report many benefits of free-writing that go beyond even the value of writing. Insights about life decisions, release of outdated beliefs and fears, and clarity about what's truly important. Try it for yourself. Here are a few important instructions for how to free-write your shaggy first draft with joy and ease.

◇ Set a timer for 5, 10 or 15 minutes.
◇ Use a prompt from your mind map or outline.
◇ Don't stop writing, not even once, during the set time.
◇ Write with the intention of exploration, not perfection.
◇ Don't judge your free-writes. You are writing a shaggy first draft. Editing will come later.
◇ Go with what comes up. It might not be what you expect.
◇ Remember to keep your reader in mind—write in your conversational tone.
◇ Don't worry about spelling, punctuation, or grammar. Phew!

You can write your entire book this way. Just go through and get a shaggy version of each chapter down. It may not be complete and it may not be "good enough," but you will have something you can work with. If you get stuck, follow the prompt *"What I really want to say . . ."*

I wrote each of these chapters in short, shaggy bursts. Each one was totally rough and incomplete. For me, it helps to have something I can sculpt, add to and revise. The second draft is where it all comes together and where the writing gets refined.

EXERCISE

Work your way through your prompts, free-writing on each item until you feel you have said everything you want to say.

ACCESS YOUR
TRUE VOICE

An odd thing happens when we sit down to write our book: it's almost like we don a formal suit and clear our throat for our "stand and deliver" moment. And what happens next? We clam up, and what had been a rich river of our material flowing through us becomes a dry and barren arroyo. When we talk about our idea or content at work or with friends, we are on fire. Nothing stops the flow of our ideas. But when we remove ourselves from the connection to others, we lose connection to our content as well. What's going on?

Some people operate better when speaking their ideas. When working with clients or teaching, the words flow. We seem to be partners with the Divine inspiration. Our thoughts flow naturally through us and out of us, reaching our audience in profound and possibly life-changing ways. But alone, at our computer, we lose connection. Instead of that great connection, we feel like we have to prove ourselves. Imposter complex creeps in and we shut down.

In our efforts to find our elusive writing voice, we seek advice to make it easier. **Sometimes being told how to write isn't as helpful as being taught how to listen.** As a professional listener, I am always attuned to what's being said and how. When you tune in, you can hear your voice become clear. I invite you to play with these ways to listen for and write from your authentic voice.

- **Get moving.** Authentic rhythms can lead us to our voice. Our bodies are completely unique, and our voice is part of that originality. Try dancing, playing, doing yoga, running, any kind of movement. Play with opening up your vocal chords while moving—see what sounds emerge and what they reveal.
- **Hearken back to hometown vernacular.** What colloquial expressions do you recall from your youth? Rice seemed to play a role in my childhood narrative. Because my father wouldn't swear, he'd substitute "Jesus Christ!" with "Cheese and rice!" Expressions from my Louisiana roots crept into my speech, my favorite being "Like white on rice."
- **Get intimate.** Think of a dear friend with whom you feel completely comfortable. With this friend, you lose any self-consciousness about how you speak. Next time you hang out, pay attention to common expressions or shortcuts you use.
- **Yuck it up.** Writing humor can be difficult, especially when you are self-conscious. Your whimsy or sardonic humor is absolutely unique to you. Humor can't be forced, but when something funny strikes you, put it down on

paper. Notice what makes you laugh and what you say that makes others laugh.

- **Love language.** Keep a list of your favorite words. What you love can lead you to recognizing and appreciating your identity and your voice. Notice what patterns appear on your list.

- **Shed the suit.** Loosen up. Get casual to tap your real voice—you may even discover that your voice rings with formality!

- **Practice.** Any authentic expression requires a lot of practice. Waiting in the wings until you find your voice won't bring it out; playing and exploring will. Write a full page of nonsense. Draft insult poems, list poems, rap poems— anything that frees you up.

- **Think about different versions of yourself.** Wild, untamed you. Sacred, deep you. Know-it-all, bossy you. Access the part of you that's deeply connected to your material and turn the pen over to her.

- **Groove with the music.** What songs make you sway and groove? What words would you use to describe your musical taste? Do any of those words apply to your voice?

- **Listen to yourself.** Record yourself reading a piece you have written, or speak your thoughts into a recorder. Listen, then take note of anything that strikes you. Hearing yourself will allow you to recognize your rhythms and verbal tics.

- **Release your passion.** Our voice emerges when

we address something we are truly committed to and fired up about. Identify and engage with what ignites you, and your voice won't be far away.

How do you know when you have found your voice? It's not as distant as you think. Yet it's one of those difficult-to-define elements that you may chase for years.

For me, when I am writing from my voice, I hear it in my head, I feel it in the pace of my fingers, I express it in the sway of my body. I also feel nervous about putting it out there. **When I fear what others think about my writing, I know I have tapped into something that's true to me.** The pieces I write from that place are the ones my readers resonate with the most.

— INQUIRY —

What helps you access your true voice?

Speak Your Book

Some of my clients have found that they speak more freely than they write. It's easier for them to speak their ideas aloud, especially when they have an audience like students or clients. The thought of sitting down and doing the work is difficult for them, more than others who consider themselves writers. It doesn't have to be difficult! One of my clients realized he could make quicker progress if he spoke his content. Using his table of contents, he would open up his dictation software and speak his book. He "wrote" his entire book this way and had a blast doing it. You can try this for yourself.

I wrote some of this book using voice dictation. For sections that I didn't feel ease with, I would simply speak my words and then revise them later. As I suggested in "Write Your Manifesto" at the end of part four, you can use Dragon Dictation software. If you are writing in Google Docs, you can use Voice Typing. Look for it under Tools. You will still need to polish your words, but getting them out in your natural voice and rhythm will feel much easier if you find speaking to be a simpler path.

⤶ Is Your Old Material ⤷
Useful?

Perhaps you have amassed material you wrote previously that could be useful for your book. Maybe you have written a blog, class content or articles. Maybe your archives are a bunch of notes in boxes of notebooks.

We might think "There's treasure in the attic!" Our archived work can feel valuable to us. But the old material may not be as useful as we think. I would place money on the odds that there isn't much value in the old writing. The majority of my clients have gone back to the archives, waded through the papers and files only to get distracted, disoriented and even disheartened.

I went back to some material I wrote over the past 20 years that I thought would be useful for this book. Certainly, various newsletters, blogs and course materials would apply, right? Alas, most of the old work wasn't useful. It was either outdated, needed a lot of revising or just didn't fit the tone of this book. Some of it was salvageable and I did copy it into the book. But it still needed a good deal of revising and reformatting.

If you are writing a memoir, your journals may have important details that will help make your writing specific and vivid. You may also draw from your note-books to get a sense of the timeline of your story. Use your reference materials to support your writing rather than hoping archives will save you from writing fresh words. Most of our archived material belongs just there—in the archives. If you feel a need to go back in and see if it's useful, by all means do so. Each case will be different. You will be able to tell on a read-through if the old content flows well with the new material you have written.

Here's my challenge: limit the amount of time you spend reviewing old material. You don't want to get stuck in the archives. It's all too easy to waste time reading old things versus writing new material. If you are as connected to your topic as I think you are, the writing you do now will be relevant, fresh and easier to get out than excavating and revising old material.

EXERCISE

Review and vet your old material. Make a decision about what will be included in the book and what will be left in the archives. Be sure that any old material follows the same format and voice as the rest of your book.

MANAGING TANGENTIAL MATERIAL

You know a lot about your topic, and there are times you may drift away from your outline as you are writing.

When we write freely, we can veer off on tangents that aren't strictly adhering to the main point. My clients often stress about wasting time writing random material that may or may not go in their book. What they don't realize is:

- We may have to go off target to get to our main point.
- Much of our writing will be warm-up throat clearing or preparatory writing.
- Some of our tangential writing can be useful in other ways.

When we publish our books, there are many opportunities to promote the book and let people know about it. We hate to feel salesy or put ourselves out there about our book. Yet all this extra material that we have been writing may be just the thing to help get the word out. Additional writing could be used for blog posts, sales copy, ad copy or other uses.

If you find that you have material that may or may not belong in the book, save it, each piece in its own document. Make a title for each so it's easy to find what you need when you search later. Perhaps put the material in a folder called "Extras from book" or "Cut from book." This way, if there are indeed gems in those pieces, you can access them later. They could be repurposed as:

◇ Stand-alone blog posts.
◇ Tweets.
◇ A basis for a freebie, a PDF or quiz that relates to your book.
◇ Material for Facebook or Instagram posts.
◇ Bonus materials for readers that you host on your website.

All of the writing itself might not be useful, but there may be a turn of phrase or sentence that sings and clearly reflects what you want your readers to know about your book. In the end, you could wind up with a collection of useless material.

My clients and I like cutting and saving our tangential material. This makes pruning our writing feel less final—we have saved it somewhere "just in case," but it's not cluttering up the book.

EXERCISE

Make a plan for managing tangential material. Keep a list of ideas in your author notebook.

Capture Promotional Ideas While Writing

This isn't a book about how to promote your book, but you may already be thinking of ways to sell your book. You may also be feeling the "ick factor" about pushing your book on people. Although you may not have the bandwidth to build a big marketing campaign while you are writing the book, there are ways you can easily capture and organize things from your book that can be used when it comes time to spread the word.

Designate in your notebook a section for marketing ideas and plans. Like the research process, the marketing process can overtake your writing time, so don't get carried away delving into details. Check out the following marketing ideas and make your own list as you read along.

- Look for memorable phrases and sentences as you write—those powerful statements that sum up your message. Consider how you can use these as posts on social media. Alongside a picture or with the colors of your book's cover, these catchphrases will help carry your message and pique interest in your book. These phrases might be the talking points you refer to when you are on podcasts or speaking about your book. **When you write something that zings, highlight it in your document so you can easily pull it out to share elsewhere.** A side benefit of capturing these is that you will notice when your writing could be more clear and concise. Watch for long sentences. Shorter sentences or those varied in length are easier for the reader to read, remember and repeat.

- Feature the basic concept of your book on your blog. The content could be your book's introduction or a chapter that lays out your main premise. This would be considered "cornerstone content" that's evergreen and tells the reader what your blog is about. You could share your manifesto on your blog. You may also be writing guest posts for others' blogs.
- Make quizzes or tests using concepts in the book as a fun way to engage readers in your material. Most of us like to learn more about ourselves. Think about how a piece of your content could be turned into a way to engage with your reader.
- Set up a simple web page to collect names and email addresses from those who are interested in your book. You can offer a short bit of content, such as the table of contents or a bit of the introduction. Keep it short—one paragraph

should do it. Just enough to spark interest for the book.

- Return to your book's themes. At the beginning of this book, I talked about how books are conversation leaders. The content of your book is the thing you want to talk about with the world. What are the themes that your book addresses? How can you write things that come from those themes? Make a quick list of five themes in your book. Write a heartfelt essay/ short piece relating to one of these themes. Use it in a newsletter or blog to lead into a conversation with the readers *before* making the ask to buy your book. Make it a wee love letter about your theme or topic. Talk *from* the book and its power rather than *about* the book.

You will come up with all kinds of ways to share your book's message that are meaningful and appropriate for you and your book. Remember to gather them in one place in your notebook as you write.

EXERCISE

Designate a space in your notebook or digital files for promotional ideas that pop up as you write. Keep them in one place and it will be easier to make a plan for using them when the time is right.

Who Wants to
Hear This?

At some point in your writing process, you will likely hear a voice in your head that says, "Who wants to hear this?" It's often not a real question but an insecurity jab, a common doubt about whether something deserves to be included. When you have those thoughts, check and see which part of you is having them. Confident author? Insecure author? If it's not the inner critic, take an honest look at how your reader will benefit. When you know your reader's needs very well, it will be easier to assess what to keep and what to jettison. With your reader in mind, you will to know what will resonate with them. When confronted with insecurities about what to include, ask yourself:

- How can you elevate your material?
- How, specifically, might this information serve your reader?
- What do you add to give it context, meaning and perspective?
- How could you make it even more useful for your reader?

Frequently, when reaching for the delete key, that's when we are writing our best stuff. Let it rip, and trust that you can edit later. In your first draft, don't edit out your material too quickly. Over time, learn how to distinguish between your inner critic's fears and legitimate concerns about what's useful material.

Exercise

Develop a short phrase or sentence to keep you going when your insecurities about whether something deserves to be included gets in the way. Some examples:

> "Just keep going."
> "Worry about quality for later drafts."
> "Writing my shaggy first draft!"

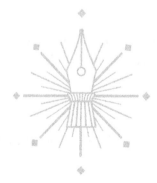

Ꮹ WEAVE IN STORIES Ꮹ

If you are like me, you may be tempted to write out your content in its conceptual form. For instance, say you are writing a how-to book. You will have numerous specific guidelines you want to get across. You just want to lay them out clearly and simply. But many readers love stories.

In her book *Wired for Story*, Lisa Cron talks about how our minds are wired to perk up when a narrative example is thrown in. This is definitely the trend with nonfiction books. We like stories or case studies to illustrate the points being made.

I am on the fence about stories. I usually want to write out the information and make it easy for readers to get the information and go do the work. I also tend to skip many of the stories in the books I read. I read quickly and want to glean the goodies without getting bogged down in the examples. For this book, I wanted it to be short and sweet. I wanted you to be able to dip in, get the information and inspiration, and get back to writing.

You may be the opposite. You might have loads of stories and fewer instructional bits for your book. In either case, here's a way to bring both in. Take a look at your outline. In a new document, create two columns. In one column, list the concepts or instructional parts from your outline. In the other column, list the stories you'd like to share related to your book's topic. If you teach or consult on your subject, you probably find yourself relating the same stories to students or clients. These stories could be of interest to your reader too, and they may belong in your book. Look to pair your instructions with examples. What stories from your life or work come to mind when you read the instructional parts?

When you have both columns filled in, it will then be easy to weave the stories into the instructional parts, or vice versa. Keep your lists handy so you can add more stories as they cross your path.

Where you put the stories will depend on your chapter template. Do you put the stories at the beginning and then add the instructions? Or weave them in after laying the foundation of your concepts? Try several ways and see what feels right for you and your book's content. You will know what's right when you try different options and read them back to yourself.

EXERCISE

Create a two-column list or use another approach to jot stories and anecdotes you might pair with the instructional/informative parts of your book. Determine how they will flow with the other material in your chapters.

Make a Punch List to Sort through a Messy Draft

Writing a book is messy, even for seasoned authors. Wrangling your material into cohesive shape is real work. There will be times when you sag with despair and cry out "This is a mess!" Rest assured. This is normal. This is not a function of your ineptitude, the lameness of your book or your inability to pull it all together. It's part of the process of writing a book. Take a deep breath and trust yourself. Let's look at how to sort this mess out. Be patient; it might take some time.

Depending on where you are with the process, it might be helpful to print out the book. Many of us are writing in one long, on-screen document. Scrolling can be a nightmare, and rolling back and forth can contribute to your feeling of chaos. If you have a draft, even a shaggy draft, print the whole thing. Make sure that the pages are 1.5- or double-spaced, with page numbers at the bottom. Reviewing a printed copy makes it so much easier to see the whole. When I went through my printed draft, it was clear that the table of contents needed to be reordered.

With your printed manuscript in hand, step away from the computer. Take your notebook and pen with you. Your plan is to make a "punch list" of things to work on next. This is a term borrowed from the construction industry, where there's a walk-through of a house before it's finished or before a sale. The punch list includes things to fix or work on. Make a punch list for your book. You want one list that you can work through methodically later.

Now, back to the messy draft. Read through everything you have written. This read-through is for the purpose of seeing the whole, for distinguishing what's working and what's missing. Read like a teacher who wants to help the student make this paper as good as possible. Put check marks, smiley faces or stars next to things that are working. Add to your punch list as needed. Avoid getting caught up in wordsmithing: if you see sentences that you want to revise, underline them or circle words you want to change, but don't get caught in the details now. Include the bigger things to work on, not the details. These could include:

- Revise chapter two.
- Add examples for chapter ten.
- Research for chapter four.
- Brainstorm ideas for images in the book.
- Identify passages that need to be fleshed out.

Your punch list will likely be long. Don't despair. It's good to have an objective list of things you can work on. The draft will still be messy, but now you have marching orders of what to improve. **This kind of list serves as a project manager.**

For each writing session, go to the list and do some of the tasks. Check them off the list to feel a sense of progress. Address as many items on your punch list as you can in each sitting, but know your limits. Notice when you feel "done" writing—you might be getting impatient, rushing and lowering your standards to make progress. The list can also keep you from feeling ambushed by emotions that may arise when you sit down to write. You are just working your way through the list. You might go through this process many times, at least once for each draft. It's okay—it helps you to know what to do when.

Exercise

When you have completed a draft, make a punch list of items to work on. Organize the items so the list is easy for you to work through.

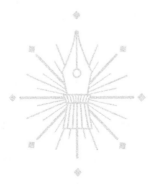

❦ REVISE AND REFINE ❧

So you have your shaggy first draft. Whoo-hoo! Time to celebrate. And then, revise and refine. This second draft is where the real work of writing happens. You will polish each sentence to truly articulate your thoughts. You will ensure that each paragraph and chapter is complete, with your ideas flowing smoothly from one to the next.

Here's the process I use to revise and refine my articles and books. Adapt it to suit your needs.

First, I make sure the book is properly formatted. For me, that means 1.5 line spacing. (You can do double-spacing if you want more space to revise on the page.) The font is 12-point Arial, with the chapter titles in bold. No fancy fonts! Leave the creativity to the writing. I also make sure that each page is numbered. This is easy to do in Word and Google Docs. In the footer, I put my name and the book's title. Seeing the title on each page reinforces that the book is coming to life. Finally, I check to see that the chapter titles on the table of contents match the chapter titles at the beginning of each chapter.

Once the manuscript is formatted, I print it double-sided. This saves paper and makes for a manuscript that's easy to carry with me. Some people put their manuscript in a three-ring binder or have it printed and bound at the printer. I like to keep the pages loose in case I need to move things around. It may seem old school to print up the book, but I see so much more on the printed page than on the screen. I edit much better on paper too.

I also like being able to take the book out and away from the screen. I have edited books on the beach, in the park, at cafés and on top of mountains. Using a colored pen that's easy to read, I make notes on the pages. If you were to see my ink, you would see *a lot* of edits on my first shaggy draft. As I mentioned, this is where the work gets refined. I don't despair that there are many changes here. It's normal and even exciting to see my work improving. I also have my notebook or a digital document alongside to make notes on bigger things to change. Keeping these notes in one place gives me the punch list I referred to in the prior chapter.

I read the entire manuscript, making notes on the pages and on my punch list. This helps me get a sense of the whole, and I am able to see what's missing. I resist the desire to go into the digital document and make changes yet. This can lead to micro-editing and getting caught in an editing sinkhole. One of the biggest traps people fall into is endlessly editing the first 30 pages. We seek to make the beginning as well written as we can and then get stuck. Don't fall into this trap! Beware the perfectionism inner critic. This is the voice that keeps you from doing anything that isn't perfect. Remember that the creative process is messy and that you will polish multiple drafts over time. **Perfect is the enemy of beginning.**

After I have read the manuscript and made notes,

I take some time away from the book. When I return, with pages in hand, I go back to the computer and enter my changes. I will likely revise and refine while doing this part, going through the whole book, adding what's needed and deleting what's not.

I repeat this process, revising and refining, as many times as necessary until I have a completed book ready to send into the world. I usually do four or five drafts of a book this way. For me, hiring an editor and putting a deadline on the calendar helps me not peck the life out of the manuscript. If you are the type of person who will endlessly edit, create a deadline for yourself to be sure to stop the process somewhere.

Have patience. Writing a book takes time and focus—and it might take many drafts. This book went through six drafts. My novel took 17 drafts. Do whatever it takes to make the book's message shine.

EXERCISE

Print the first draft of your manuscript. Read through and revise. Revise and refine again.

— INQUIRY —

What, specifically, is "good enough" for you regarding your book? What's exciting to you about the revision process?

DESIGN THE FEEDBACK PROCESS

There comes a time when we want feedback on our writing. Are we going in the right direction? Do our ideas actually make sense and hang together? When we are immersed in writing, it's hard to have what I call critical distance, and we may not feel like we are saying exactly what we want. Then later, when we reread our words, we realize we *have* actually gotten something good out.

The key word here's *feel*. Though our feelings are important and helpful in work and life, sometimes they can get in the way of our writing. By feelings, I mean the feelings *about* the work. It's easy to slip under the influence of the inner critic or editor, and that's not always the best part of ourselves to listen to. If we write with too much self-criticism, there's a good chance our work will be drained of our voice and our vitality.

I take the feedback process very seriously. It can be either destructive or constructive. I have seen how feedback can devastate people and annihilate their creative dreams. It's awful. Yet feedback is a necessary part of succeeding as a writer or artist, so it's wise to design a process that's constructive, not destructive. You may start with getting feedback on a chapter or two. This can help you know if you are going in the right direction. There will come a time when you will need feedback on the entire manuscript. Here are five strategies to consider when asking for feedback on your book.

— GET YOUR TIMING RIGHT —

In many cases, we may not be truly seeking feedback but approval. We want the pat on the head that tells us how great our story is. Then our confidence is demolished when the person giving feedback shreds our writing, pointing out not our brilliance but how much work still needs to be done. We didn't get good feedback; we got decimated.

Whether you are getting feedback on one or two chapters or the whole manuscript, don't rush to solicit feedback before your work is truly ready. Be sure you are prepared to hear others' opinions. How do you know when you are ready to share your work with someone? See how many of the following scenarios apply to you and your book.

◇ You have done as much work as you can, have stepped back and assessed your project. You know you need pointers on where to go next.

◇ You are eager to make the work as good as you can and are willing and able to hear opinions that may not match yours.

◇ You know something is off but aren't sure what.

◇ You know what's missing and want feedback to confirm your intuition.

◇ You want an objective opinion about your piece.

Do you want ego stroking or a genuine critique? Be clear about your motives for soliciting feedback. Then give your work a thorough once-over before handing it off to someone else.

── SEEK FEEDBACK FROM THE RIGHT SOURCES ──

One thing that can turn the creative process into a disaster is asking the wrong people for feedback. Doing this limits our chances of getting constructive and kind feedback. Who aren't the right people? Spouses, parents and children may not be objective enough to give useful comments. They may not want to hurt our feelings, or at the other end, they may be insensitive to our feelings. A spouse or a friend may have no clue about what makes good writing, and they just don't have the skills to comment.

Even a seemingly benign comment like "That's nice, honey" can have a negative impact. A client of mine showed her husband her essay, and he—thinking he was being nice—said, "That's great. You could write a book about that." While that may seem like an encouraging comment, it's not reflective of what's in the essay. It doesn't point the writer to specific ways she can improve the piece. Turning the piece into something bigger may be helpful in the future, but it doesn't give her constructive feedback for the work as it is.

Who are the right people to give feedback? Seek trusted creative peers, mentors, or teachers who have your best interests in mind. I have hired editors to give me feedback, knowing that they had a level of professionalism and would give me straight, constructive feedback.

DESIGN THE PROCESS WITH YOUR GOALS IN MIND

Don't do your work the disservice of handing it off to someone without specific requests. You have more power in the feedback process than you think. Never give someone your work and ask, "What do you think?" That vague question will lead to vague or overly enthusiastic feedback. Sometimes the giver's ego can get a little inflated. Here's their chance to be right, to know and to point out all the things that are wrong with your project. And if you send a stranger this request, chances are you will never hear from that person again.

ACKNOWLEDGE AND DEAL WITH EMOTIONS

No matter how tough you are and how much you want to hear commentary, doing so can still be an emotional landmine. **Give yourself time to integrate the emotions that arise when facing a critique.** You may be in denial, you may want to argue, or you may be hurt or frustrated that you still have a lot of work to do. Set the feedback aside until at least the next day. Talk a walk, exercise, talk it out with a friend, jot some notes about how you feel.

Trust me, muscling past these emotions will only cause them to explode later. And knowing how you feel about the feedback will help to discern what's useful and what's not. Then, when you feel more objective, take a look at the feedback. You will need a clear mind to determine what's useful, which is the next critical phase.

— SORT THROUGH FOR WHAT'S USEFUL —

You have gotten your feedback and now need to discern what will improve your book. How do you know what's useful? Make notes as you go through the feedback. Make a list of possible revision actions. Being as objective as you can, look at the feedback and ask, "What's true?" Keep your original objective in mind about your project and use that as a guidepost for whether the feedback you have received will be integrated or discarded.

Another question to ask is, "What can I learn here?" Notice if defensiveness arises and fend it off. That's usually a reaction that masks your feelings and doesn't allow room for improvement. If you can't move past defensiveness, write down your arguments and be sure you are following a good hunch and not massaging a bruised ego.

Constructive commentary is an essential part of the creative success, and if you are interested in improving your work, you should seek feedback regularly. But it doesn't have to decimate your work and your creative dreams. Do it right and feedback can build, not destroy, your creative dreams.

EXERCISE

Identify beta readers. These are usually people who represent your ideal reader. Choose a few people who have expressed interest in your book and who are willing to read an early draft. Then, do your part to solicit useful feedback. Before you hand over your precious material, take these steps:

1. Know your goal or desired outcome for the book. You have already determined the impact you want the book to have on the reader.

2. Clarify what kind of feedback would best serve you. (Glowing praise surely, but dig a little deeper.) Do you want micro-critiquing? If so, let your reader know you want them to zero in on word choices, sentence structure, and other line-editing details. Or is big-picture feedback enough? If you are looking for a detailed critique that involves the micro and the macro, be sure to let your critic know.

3. Tell your reader what your book's goal is. Ask them to say whether you have achieved your aim. If not, what's missing? What's working that could be amplified?

4. Decide how you want the news. Verbally? Written? If you get the feedback verbally, record it or have someone else take notes. When you listen to the feedback, you will process the information on many levels. If you won't be distracted making notes while listening, it will be much easier to absorb the feedback this way. You may prefer the comments in written form. A written critique will be easier to assess later.

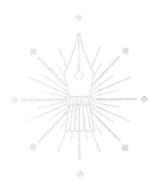

PAY FOR PROFESSIONAL PRODUCTION HELP

You have received feedback from your teacher, coach, developmental editor or beta readers. You have spent the time to revise as much as you can (this could take months), and the book feels finished. It's time to seek professional copy editing. This is a step many self-published authors skip, and it shows in their pages. When you have done the best you can with your draft, when you don't see how to make it any better, it's time to bring in a copy editor. This is someone you pay to read carefully through the book and make sure it's consistent, clear, and free of errors.

A copy editor corrects grammatical and spelling errors, addresses inconsistencies, and ensures that the text flows clearly and makes sense. They will likely have questions and comments for you too. Having a good rapport with your editor is essential. This person should understand your topic and even be excited about your book. When you can find an editor who cares about you, your topic and your book's success, all the better.

After you have integrated the copy editor's changes and have addressed their comments, you are ready to work with a professional book designer. Once the designer has laid out the book, it's time to hire a proofreader. This person makes corrections on a printout or in a PDF. The proofreader ensures that no errors have been overlooked before the final pages go to the printer. In some cases, a back-of-the-book index is beneficial. If that's true for your book, you would hire an indexer *after* the pages have been proofread and updated by the designer.

Do not skimp on any of these professionals because they will help make your book as good as it can be. Expect to invest in these parts of the publication process. To find good editors, designers, proofreaders and indexers, look to your network first. Ask your author friends who they hired to work on their books. Post on your social media channels, clearly describing what you are looking for. Some authors will want to work with a company that can help them get their book out via POD or an e-book.

When preparing to publish, consider that your book is your new business. It's going to require its own promotional process. Authors are often tired of the book just when it's time to talk about it everywhere. This is when help will be needed to ensure that you are doing as much as you can to give your book a chance in the world. Getting help managing things like social media campaigns, podcast guest pitching and other approaches is a good idea.

If hiring and managing freelancers is not your thing, working with a company that offers self-publishing services may be the way to go. The Alliance of Independent Authors posts an updated list of companies that serve authors. "The Best and Worst Self-Publishing Services Reviewed and Rated by the Alliance of Independent Authors" is a great resource for reputable support. However, I still recommend hiring a professional editor first to ensure that the manuscript reads as well as it can.

EXERCISE

Get recommendations from friends or industry experts for editing and other book production support. If needed, start saving money for this important investment.

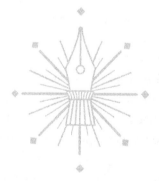

ᕤ WRITE YOUR ᕤ
ACKNOWLEDGMENTS PAGE

There comes a point in the writing of your book when it's just a slog. You are close to the end but you don't feel like you will ever see that finish line or hold your book in your hands. This creative despair can be crippling. Time to lighten things up with gratitude. One way to amplify gratitude is to write your acknowledgments page. This page isn't just a nicety. Finishing a book really does require the help of numerous people. Even though your name is on the cover, the names on the acknowledgments page are equally important, especially when you need to gather encouragement.

You may not be able to invite these people over to soothe your writer's soul, but you can bring them together by drafting your acknowledgments page. When I drafted my acknowledgments page for my novel, I nearly wept with gratitude. As I listed my editors, readers, teachers and champions, I felt their support around me. I recalled their words of encouragement and basked in their belief in my book. I also panicked a bit, fearing I would leave someone out! But I had started the list early enough that I could add names as needed. It, like my book, is a living document, evolving over time.

Try this for your book. Add to it whenever you need an extra boost. Keep the list present so you can glean ongoing support—and add more names.

EXERCISE

Write your acknowledgments page. Make it yours, make it heartfelt, and let it be something that keeps you inspired.

Overcome Obstacles and Finish Your Book

Ah, you are finally at the finish line! You have written several drafts (at least three, probably more), gotten feedback from your ideal reader and had the book professionally edited. You had momentum and now things have ground to a halt or a drag. It's somehow more difficult to focus on the book.

It's usually the last 20 percent of the book— or any project—that is the most difficult. We are at the place where it's as good as it's going to be, and we have to face the limitations of our abilities and skills. We are closer to bringing it out into the world, and that is scary. **Bringing our work to our audience is a true threshold.** We want so much for our readers and we want to meet their expectations and ensure that we have done the very best we can. We see the finish line and we know what's needed to complete the project. But emotions rise up and threaten to throw us off course. We can't let the inner critic take control now. Watch out for these things that will try to derail your completion:

> ❧ **Crises of confidence.** You may experience
> these frequently, feeling uncertain, unclear and

unmotivated. The trick is to just keep showing up for your writing dates, no matter how you feel about them. Our feelings are important, and often in the writing process, they overtake our rational minds. We don't feel like writing. We don't feel like we know what we are saying. We don't feel clear about the path forward. Guess what? The path forward is just straight through. Keep showing up, keep using your outline and free-writing process, and you will make progress.

- **Future tripping.** Sometimes we get caught up thinking about marketing or design issues before we have written enough on the book. It's important to consider those parts of the process, but until you have a complete manuscript, your book doesn't exist to be marketed or designed. Notice when you start thinking about future scenarios. It could be that you are avoiding the hard work of writing the next good sentence. And then the next one and the next.

- **Loud inner critic.** You hear its voice more than the voice that motivates you. It tries to point out ways you have been a non-finisher in the past. When we reach the limit of our beliefs about ourselves and what's possible, we throw up barricades and cause problems for ourselves. Gay Hendricks describes this as our "upper limit." He writes about this in his book *The Big Leap*, which was a world-changing book for me.

- **Deep fear.** I have felt such primal, deep fear before finishing and launching a book. Even a book that's not solving world hunger feels massively important, and thus deadly risky. Maybe the bigger picture of your dream is actually holding you back. Maybe you fear some of the changes that you suspect will happen when you finish your book. Try this. Make a scale of importance. On one end is life threatening: if you do this, it will kill you. On the other end: if you do this, it will bring you all the riches and fame you ever dreamed of. Both are probably unlikely, but our fears make us operate on these extreme assumptions. Go for something in the middle: writing this is important enough for you to spend your time on. Give it your all and release expectations of grandeur or failure.

- **Decision swirl.** You may have found yourself caught in indecisiveness, unsure about how to move forward on your book. Indecision can show up as endless editing, especially without a feedback loop to help you move forward. Don't think you have to go back and rework your entire table of contents. Instead, identify the next step. It's okay if it's not the *best* step or the *right* step. Just commit to continued action. Trust that if you keep showing up, you will be able to sort it out or get help to do so. You have got this. It's time. Finish your book and savor the fruits of your labor.

Be sure you have the support you need for the final pages. Your writing buddies, your writing coach, your allies can all help you now. This may not feel as exciting as the beginning phase of writing the book, but it's much more powerful. This is where you claim the authority you have earned and are bringing it out into the world.

The final phase before the finish line is the real test. It can be unbelievably hard! My hope is that sharing some of the obstacles you may encounter will normalize them if you experience some of these roadblocks. If you find yourself caught in a creative cul-de-sac and are unable to finish your book, you may benefit from an e-book I wrote, *Cross the Finish Line: Overcome the Obstacles to Completion.*

— INQUIRY —

What will help you overcome the obstacles to finishing?

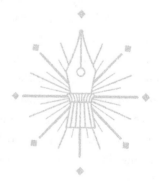

⮾ Parting Note ⮾

I hope this book has offered at least *one* thing that is useful to get you started and help you complete your book. Ideally, it has given you a road map to bring your material into book form. It has helped you move with grace past hurdles. And it has offered you a way to embrace the challenging and rewarding process of writing a book.

The last thing you may want to hear is that it will take time to write your world-changing book. Sure, there are workshops promising to help you write your book in a weekend. Be wary of such hype. A book is a big project and takes focus, heart, smart and soul to make it happen. It doesn't matter how long it takes. What matters is your commitment to the book and your ability to stay focused on it. Give it everything you can, as much as you can. This will require multiple drafts. That's okay! Remember, you are in a committed relationship with this book, and you might have to renew your fervor for it a few times.

Once you have written one book, your next books will be easier. You will know your process. You will know how to settle in. You will have sorted through what works and what doesn't. Your style will be clear and your confidence strong.

May your book writing empower you. Let you meet its challenges, like a good friend who cherishes you and calls you to be your best. Let your words ring true for you and all the right readers. May your book change worlds, including, first and foremost, your own.

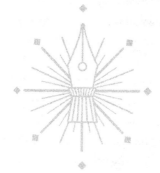

৩৩ SAMPLE PUNCH LIST ৩৩

It can help to have a list of things to review to make sure your book is complete. Here's a start. Add your own items as needed. Sometimes the punch list will be long. That's alright. Be glad you know what specifically to work on.

- ❧ I have covered everything I want in this book.
- ❧ The contents in the book match the promise in the marketing copy.
- ❧ The table of contents titles match the titles of each chapter exactly.
- ❧ The contents of each chapter meet the promise of the chapter titles.
- ❧ The book speaks to my main reader and solves one or more of their problems.
- ❧ I have done at least two drafts before asking for beta readers or professional editing.
- ❧ The spelling, punctuation and grammar have been thoroughly checked.
- ❧ I feel good about the book, its contents and the possibilities.

CHECKLIST OF EXERCISES AND INQUIRIES

These are the exercises and inquiries I have shared throughout the book. Don't fret if you don't do them all. They may be particularly useful when you feel stuck. Use what's right for you and ignore what isn't.

PART ONE: DEVELOP YOUR AUTHOR MINDSET

◇ Get a container—a notebook or computer file—that's dedicated to your book.

◇ Free-write your "why" for writing this book, and extract your rallying cry from this writing. Post your book's rallying cry where you will see it and gain strength and motivation from it.

◇ Inquiry: *What does soul work mean for you? Do you see your book as soul work?*

◇ Make a list of the conversations that might spring up around the topics in your book.

◇ Inquiry: *How will the world be different with your book in it? What do you imagine will change because of your book?*

◇ Free-write to get to the heart of which publishing path feels right for you. Then list three reasons why you chose this path.

◇ Inquiry: *What book will you start with and what makes that a good choice for you now?*

◇ Inquiry: *What does a healthy relationship with your book and author self look like on your busiest week?*

◇ Inquiry: *What do you notice about your relationship with time and your book? What do you hear yourself saying and thinking about time or lack of it?*

◇ Mind-map your plate, listing your current obligations and projects.

◇ Inquiry: *Are you able and willing to commit space to making your book a priority?*

◇ Write a character sketch of your inner critic.

◇ Inquiry: *What has shifted for you as a result of getting to know your inner critic?*

◇ Inquiry: *How can your inner champion help motivate you?*

◇ Inquiry: *How can you set up your book writing so you don't feel guilty taking time from your other obligations? What will help you deflect any guilt that arises when you take time to work on your book?*

◇ Determine who your allies will be and what you will need from them.

◇ Determine who your detractors may be and how you will keep boundaries with them.

◇ Inquiry: *What will help you navigate those moments of cluelessness? Don't forget a healthy sense of humor.*

◇ At the end of each writing session, jot three words to describe your experience. Keep a running list to witness how the writing is changing you.

Part two: Get started writing

◇ Try a quick free-write. Set a timer for 10 minutes. Use the prompt "I write because . . ."

◇ Choose a timer. Experiment with 5-, 10- and 15-minute free-writing sessions. Build up your writing stride over time.

◇ Make a list of writing prompts for your book. Keep it in one single document so you can access it easily.

◇ This week, write from at least two of your prompts.

◇ Schedule eight 15-minute writing sessions in the next 30 days.

Part three: Design your writing practice

◇ What does your writing practice look like for the next 30 days? Write that down.

◇ To get back on track with your book, set up a 15-minute date: open your notebook, read what you wrote last time, make notes about what to work on next.

◇ Inquiry: *How have you been an ardent opportunist for your creative projects? For your book?*

◇ With your author notebook or pad of paper beside you when writing, capture the thoughts that intrude on your writing time by keeping two lists: ideas for the book and a list for everything else.

◇ Inquiry: *What's your idea of a "productive" session? What helps you stay focused when writing?*

◇ Identify your author zone(s).

◇ Inquiry: *What will be your approach to writing and traveling?*

◇ Inquiry: *How can you use deadlines, goals and milestones to finish your book?*

◇ Write down the practices that contribute to your book writing. Be specific about why they are vital to your creative work.

◇ Inquiry: *What's your plan for keeping your research process in balance with your writing?*

◇ Inquiry: *What have you done that you can draw upon to build your book-writing confidence?*

PART FOUR: MANAGE YOUR CONTENT

◇ Write a letter to your ideal reader to connect to them specifically and personally.

◇ Inquiry: *What resistance, if any, comes up for you when I ask you to choose a specific reader?*

◇ Make a list, or mind-map the challenges your reader has around your topic. Make sure your table of contents addresses at least five or your reader's problems.

◇ Inquiry: *What problems does your book address?*

◇ Choose one software system to write your book and stick with it.

◇ Determine the structure for your book.

◇ Mind map your material to help you clarify the content of your book.

◇ Put your mind-map into an outline form.

◇ Develop a template for your chapters, then draft a sample chapter using the elements of your template.

◇ Write short, four-sentence chapter summaries.

◇ Write the jacket copy for your book, including a one-paragraph author bio.

◇ Draft a working title for your book.

◇ Draft your book's manifesto.

Part five: Write and finish your book

◇ Inquiry: *What do you notice when you write from your prompts?*

◇ Free-write from your prompts to write your shaggy first draft.

◇ Inquiry: *What helps you access your true voice?*

◇ Decide whether to include old material in your book or leave it in the archives.

◇ Make a plan for managing tangential material that may be used elsewhere.

◇ Designate a space in your notebook or digital files for promotional ideas that pop up as you write.

◇ Develop a short phrase or sentence to keep you going when your insecurities about whether to include something get in the way.

◇   List stories and anecdotes you might pair with your instructions or information.

◇   Make a punch list of things to work on.

◇   Print the first draft of your manuscript. Read through and revise. Revise and refine again.

◇   Inquiry: *What, specifically, is "good enough" for you regarding your book? What's exciting to you about the revision process?*

◇   Identify beta readers, then design the feedback process for a chapter or two and, eventually, for the whole manuscript, before sending out your material.

◇   Hire a professional copy editor and other book-production professionals.

◇   Write your acknowledgments page.

◇   Inquiry: *What will help you overcome the obstacles to finishing?*

↶ RESOURCES ↷

There are so many resources for writing and publishing your book. I have included a few of my favorites here. This book contains some affiliate links. When you buy something from one of these links, I may receive a small percentage of the sale. For more resources, please visit OriginalImpulse.com/GuideToWritingBook.

Books

Bird by Bird: Some Instructions on Writing and Life by Anne Lamott

Writing Down the Bones: Freeing the Writer Within by Natalie Goldberg

Green-Light Your Book: How Writers Can Succeed in the New Era of Publishing by Brooke Warner

One Continuous Mistake: Four Noble Truths About Writing by Gail Sher

The Checklist Manifesto: How to Get Things Right by Atul Gawande

Writing the Breakout Novel: Insider Advice for Taking Your Fiction to the Next Level by Donald Maass

The Writer's Journey: Mythic Structure for Writers by Christopher Vogler

Big Magic: Creative Living Beyond Fear by Elizabeth Gilbert

Soulful Simplicity: How Living with Less Can Lead to So Much More by Courtney Carver

The Big Leap: Conquer Your Hidden Fear and Take Life to the Next Level by Gay Hendricks

Your Story Is Your Power: Access Your Feminine Voice by Elle Luna and Susie Herrick

How to Write a Book Proposal: The Insider's Step-by-Step Guide to Proposals That Get You Published by Jody Rein and Michael Larsen

Wired for Story: The Writer's Guide to Using Brain Science to Hook Readers from the Very First Sentence by Lisa Cron

Websites

Jane Friedman is a great resource for publishing: Jane Friedman.com

The Alliance of Independent Authors is a resource for self-publishing: SelfPublishingAdvice.org

Here are hybrid press options:
- Inkshares: Inkshares.com
- She Writes Press: SheWritesPress.com

Here are a few self-publishing vendors:
- Blurb is good for books with images or heavy formatting like cookbooks or photo books.
- Ingram Spark
- Lulu

Tools

CreaWriter is a full-screen solution for Windows users.

Dragon Anywhere is a voice recording software that you can use to speak your book aloud.

Evernote is a mobile app designed for note taking and productivity.

Grammarly is an online writing app that helps eliminate grammar errors.

Insight Timer is a meditation app that can be used for writing sessions.

Mindmeister is a digital mind-mapping software.

Omm Writer, now called Gaia, uses audio and typefaces to help create a distraction-free environment.

Rev is a transcription service that can transcribe your recordings if you speak your book aloud.

WriteRoom for the Mac helps shut down screens and tabs on your computer so you can focus on your manuscript.

❧ ACKNOWLEDGMENTS ❧

Those who have written books understand that a project of this scope is certainly done with a lot of help. I am grateful to have the support of the talented, smart people in my life who have helped me make this book the best it can be.

Thank you to my beta readers, Barbara Techel, Cindy Lusk and Karen Wright. Thanks to my great editor, Jody Berman, and the talented designers Ian Koviak and Alan Dino Hebel of The Book Designers. Thanks to Shelly Heller for helping me get this out into the world. Thank you to my proofreader, Laurel Kallenbach, who made sure everything was perfect before printing. Thanks go also to my indexer, Teresa Abney. Thanks to Darren Scanson of CCM Recording Studios for helping make the audio version of this book great. Thank you to my Atelier members, who inspired me to focus on this project. A deep bow of gratitude to all my clients who have allowed me to help them write their books. It's an honor and a privilege. Thank you to my online friends, who have encouraged me to keep going. I offer deep gratitude to my friends, colleagues and family who believe in me and in this book.

THE END

INDEX

✎ ABOUT THE AUTHOR ✎

Author and certified coach Cynthia Morris helps writers, artists and entrepreneurs focus, follow through, and finish their creative work. In 1999, she founded Original Impulse to help people become the writers they have always wanted to be. Cynthia has published seven nonfiction books and a Paris historical novel. She speaks globally on writing and the creative process and leads retreats. In her online workshops, she guides writers to get their words out, stay committed to their projects, and cross the finish line with books in hand. Resources and information about how to create your writer's life are at OriginalImpulse.com.

CPSIA information can be obtained
at www.ICGtesting.com
Printed in the USA
FSHW020958251119
64475FS